Praise for

TAKE THE STAIRS

"I always say that personal finance is only 20% head knowledge and 80% behavior. Behavior change is hard, because it requires something a lot of people are missing these days: self-discipline. If you want to make a change in your money, business, or relationships, do not miss *Take the Stairs*. It gives you the tools you need to take control of the only person holding you back: yourself."

—Dave Ramsey, host of *The Dave Ramsey Show* and bestselling author of *The Total Money Makeover*

"This book won't let you off easy—and that's why it's great. Rory Vaden gives readers what they need to get focused and tackle problems head-on—and win." —Keith Ferrazzi, bestselling author of *Never Eat Alone*

"This book shows how to develop the courage, character, and determination to succeed in anything you attempt. It can change your life!"

—Brian Tracy, bestselling author of *Eat That Frog!*

"*Take the Stairs* is a compelling and challenging call for all of us to accomplish greatness. It not only shows you how to make self-discipline more sustainable, it will reignite your passion to achieve."

—Andy Andrews, bestselling author of *The Traveler's Gift* and *The Noticer*

"A gem of a book that will inspire you to do the little extra things that make a *huge* difference. Buy it!"

—Chester Elton, bestselling coauthor of *The Orange Revolution*

"If there is one book to read this year, this might be it. It's at the core of *everything*. Brilliant. Significant. Necessary."

—Roxanne Emmerich, bestselling author of *Thank God It's Monday!*

"Motivating yourself is a key to success in all of life. Read this book and your fighting spirit will come alive!"

—Mac Anderson, founder of Simple Truths and former owner of Successories

"Don't be fooled. There is no escalator to the top. This book will tell you the truth about what it really takes to become a massive success in every area of your life—if you choose to Take the Stairs."

—Darren Hardy, publisher of *Success* magazine and bestselling author of *The Compound Effect*

continued . . .

"The easy way is never the excellent way. For get rich quick or wish upon a star, go elsewhere. For an agenda for excellence, read this book. Rory gets it."

—Mark Sanborn, bestselling author of
The Fred Factor and *You Don't Need a Title to Be a Leader*

"This isn't a book of cheerleading and motivational platitudes. This is the book that can change your life. I highly recommend it to anyone who is looking to take quality of work and life to a higher level."

—Joe Calloway, bestselling author of *Becoming a Category of One*

"Do you have a career worth loving? Rory Vaden will give you the ideas, insight, and inspiration to create a career worthy of your greatest potential."

—Sally Hogshead, author of *Fascinate* and founder of HowToFascinate.com

"Rory's book, *Take the Stairs*, is an encouraging message of hope and truth that can really help you improve your life. Read it as soon as possible!"   —Tom Ziglar, CEO of Ziglar Inc. and proud son of Zig Ziglar

"Pure and simple, this should be the only book on the shelf in this category—because it's the only proven way to achieve authentic, sustainable success. Buy this book and heed this message!"

—David Avrin, author of *It's Not Who You Know—It's Who Knows YOU!*

"An inspiring and empowering book on how to harness your potential and become great."   —Randy Gage, author of *The Prosperity Mind*

"*Take the Stairs* identifies the specific strategies that will help you get past procrastination and fear to accomplish anything you desire."

—Ron Marks, author of *Managing for Sales Results*

"You can't spend 30 seconds around Rory without getting inspired to change your life. You're about to spend a few hours with him. Get ready."

—Jon Acuff, bestselling author of *Quitter:*
Closing the Gap Between Your Day Job and Your Dream Job

TAKE THE
STAIRS

7 STEPS TO ACHIEVING TRUE SUCCESS

Rory Vaden

A Perigee Book

A PERIGEE BOOK
Published by the Penguin Group
Penguin Group (USA) Inc.
375 Hudson Street, New York, New York 10014, USA
Penguin Group (Canada), 90 Eglinton Avenue East, Suite 700, Toronto, Ontario M4P 2Y3, Canada
(a division of Pearson Penguin Canada Inc.) • Penguin Books Ltd., 80 Strand, London WC2R 0RL,
England • Penguin Ireland, 25 St. Stephen's Green, Dublin 2, Ireland (a division of Penguin
Books Ltd.) • Penguin Group (Australia), 707 Collins Street, Melbourne, Victoria 3008, Australia
(a division of Pearson Australia Group Pty Ltd.) • Penguin Books India Pvt. Ltd., 11 Community
Centre, Panchsheel Park, New Delhi—110 017, India • Penguin Group (NZ), 67 Apollo Drive,
Rosedale, Auckland 0632, New Zealand (a division of Pearson New Zealand Ltd.) • Penguin Books,
Rosebank Office Park, 181 Jan Smuts Avenue, Parktown North 2193, South Africa • Penguin China, B7
Jaiming Center, 27 East Third Ring Road North, Chaoyang District, Beijing 100020, China

Penguin Books Ltd., Registered Offices: 80 Strand, London WC2R 0RL, England

While the author has made every effort to provide accurate telephone numbers, Internet addresses, and other contact information at the time of publication, neither the publisher nor the author assumes any responsibility for errors, or for changes that occur after publication. Further, the publisher does not have any control over and does not assume any responsibility for author or third-party websites or their content.

PUBLISHING HISTORY
Perigee hardcover edition / February 2012
Perigee trade paperback edition / January 2013

Perigee trade paperback ISBN: 978-0-399-53776-9

The Library of Congress has cataloged the Perigee hardcover edition as follows:

Vaden, Rory.
Take the stairs : 7 steps to achieving true success / Rory Vaden.
p.   cm.
ISBN 978-0-399-53723-3
1. Success in business.   2. Success.   3. Self-management (Psychology)   I. Title.
HF5386.V143   2012
650.1—dc23   2011039168

PRINTED IN THE UNITED STATES OF AMERICA

10 9

Most Perigee books are available at special quantity discounts for bulk purchases for sales promotions, premiums, fund-raising, or educational use. Special books, or book excerpts, can also be created to fit specific needs. For details, write: Special Markets, Penguin Group (USA) Inc., 375 Hudson Street, New York, New York 10014.

*This book is dedicated to the two most
important women in my life:*

*To Mom, thank you for the sacrifices you made to raise
Randy and me up in truth, and for making sure we always
had extravagant love even though we had little money.*

*To my precious wife, Amanda. You are the reason that
I live and the reason God created me. You are the
most abundant blessing in my life. Thank you for being my
partner through it all.*

CONTENTS

Waking Up in a ProcrastiNation

The last time you came up to a set of stairs and an escalator, did you *Take the Stairs*? If you're like 95% of the world, then you probably didn't. Most people don't; most of the time we look for shortcuts. We all want to be successful and we all want to have a happy life, but we constantly look for the easy way. We look for the "escalator" in hopes that life will be easier. Unfortunately, in our search for making things easier, we are actually making them worse.

Americans are failing. Health data shows that 66% of adults in our country are overweight and 31% are obese. The divorce rate for our first marriages is 41% with the rate for second marriages soaring to 60%. There were over 800,000 of us who filed for nonbusiness bankruptcy recently, and an estimated 46.6 million of us are smokers.

Are You Affected by Any of These Problems?

I certainly am, and so are the people I love. And while some of us make these choices deliberately, for many of us our lives have strayed from our original intentions. People are failing. Not by my standards, but by their own.

In many key areas of life we are simply missing the mark. Central to all of these challenges is a lack of one value that is diminishing in modern culture: self-discipline. We live in a "get rich quick" society where we can "lose weight fast" or cure our ailments by "asking our doctor about the next magic pill." But there is a huge invisible cost to living in our shortcut society.

We are conditioned to believe that it is moral to pursue immediate satisfaction and that difficulties can always be circumvented. We don't want to make any sacrifices, and for many of us we have never had to. Instead, the vast majority of Western societies have adopted an "escalator mentality"—one that says getting what we want shouldn't require much work, and that there are always shortcuts in business and in life.

The problem is that the escalator mind-set is crushing our

confidence and paralyzing the very actions it takes to truly become successful.

We have no accountability because we all allow each other to get away with debt, indulgence, and procrastination. We want everything now and we want it without earning it. We've come to expect dessert to be served to us without having to finish our dinner. We almost never finish things that we start; at least not if they aren't convenient or comprehensively entertaining.

For example, there's a great chance that you won't finish reading this book. At least not cover to cover. If you're like most people in the world today, then you have read fewer than five books cover to cover in your lifetime. According to one major American publisher, 95% of all books that are purchased are never completely read. And congratulations if you've made it this far, because 70% of all books ever purchased are never even opened!

Instead of reading the book, we'd rather get the CliffsNotes. Instead of changing our diets, we'd rather get the latest fitness contraption. Instead of budgeting our money, we'd rather play the lottery or charge up our credit cards. Overall, most of us belong to the school of thought that asks, "Why would I take the stairs when I could just take the escalator?"

> We almost never finish things that we start; at least not if they aren't convenient or comprehensively entertaining.

Every one of us is searching for shortcuts. In most

everything we do. We're basically programmed that way because the idea of shortcuts is being sold to us through almost every major medium in the world. We see magazine ads that tell us "how to lose weight in 4 minutes a day," and we buy books that promise us the chance to think and *attract* success to come to us without us having to do a darn thing.

There are game shows that test our own greed through our willingness to backstab other human beings for the chance to make millions or become a reality TV star. There are pills, books, magazines, speakers, contraptions, and jigamaroos sold to us to make our lives easier in all areas, because—let's face it—it's easy to be just one more guy out there who is looking for "the secret." We're looking for the easy way—the way where things will come to us so we don't have to go out and work.

> I'm not prepared to leave my life's success up to chance. Are you?

I enjoyed some of those game shows, I tried some of those same magic pills, and I subscribed to some of those same beliefs about success. But then I woke up one day feeling like I had been brainwashed because, without realizing it, my mind had changed to think I could somehow have it all without discipline, sacrifice, or hard work.

The only problem with always looking for shortcuts is that most of us aren't going to win *American Idol*, the lottery, or *Deal or No Deal*. It's rare that you or someone you know will make it as a big star in Hollywood, the NBA, or the Olympics. So while there are some great gimmicks out there and some great success stories, the idea of betting on becoming an "overnight success" doesn't seem like a sound plan to live by. I'm not prepared to leave my life's success up to chance. Are you?

Despite many well-crafted marketing messages, the formula for success is no secret. It has just been long forgotten in our world of excess, and it's so obvious that it's elusive. The only guaranteed formula to succeed in anything is the same as it has always been.

Around the house growing up, my family always promoted success because my mom and my brother would always tell me, "One day, Ror, you're going to grow up and you're going to make it!" I wanted success so I started studying it. I got a degree in leadership, management, and an MBA. While in college I just so happened to get recruited into one of the world's most intensive training programs on success for young people: the Southwestern Company.

Southwestern taught me the true principles of business and personal success that have enabled them to create an entire family of companies over the past 150 years and literally hundreds of the world's top leaders. Southwestern was a culture that bred success and it not only exposed me to life principles but also gave me a platform to build my own half-million-dollar business while still in college. There I became infatuated with what made people successful.

I started meeting and interviewing successful people from

walks of life. I read dozens of books from the most success-ful people in the world. I spent thousands of dollars on courses and spent countless hours thinking about one inescapable question: "What makes successful people successful?"

Later, I even cofounded a multimillion-dollar international training company called Southwestern Consulting, which puts on large motivational success conferences. We have tens of thousands of successful people come through our training. We coach hundreds of the most successful salespeople and entrepreneurs in the United States. Now I keynote at corporate events for top organizations all around the world, and what I have learned is that there is one thing that *all* successful people have in common: Successful people have all had to do things they didn't feel like doing in order to get where they are.

Success isn't easy. Success isn't overnight. Success isn't ordinary. And so becoming successful requires us to do things that aren't easy and things that people don't *ordinarily* do. Success means we have to develop the self-discipline to get ourselves to do things we don't want to do. In other words, success is not about taking the escalator— it's about taking the stairs.

> Successful people have all had to do things they didn't feel like doing in order to get where they are.

Successful people have the self-discipline to do things they don't want to do. They do the things they don't want to do *even when* they don't *feel like* doing them. Discipline is mandatory if we want to control our own success because most of the time success requires activities that we wouldn't usually *want* to do. But there is good news . . .

Doing things we don't feel like doing isn't as hard as we think—when we know how to think the right way. It's not that successful people find it easier to do things that most people don't like doing; it's that they think differently about it. This book shows us how to think like successful people think in order that we may do as successful people do so that we can have the things that successful people have.

What would you have if you could have anything? What if you could have it by simply learning to change the way you think? Well, you can.

Take the Stairs is about self-discipline—the ability to take action regardless of your emotional state, financial state, or physical state. This book isn't about doing things the hardest way possible, but it *is* about doing the hardest things as soon as possible so that you can get whatever you want in life—as soon as possible.

Imagine what you could accomplish if you could get yourself to follow through on your best intentions no matter what. Picture yourself saying to your body, "You're overweight. Lose twenty pounds (or more)." Without solid self-discipline, that intention won't become a reality. But with sufficient self-discipline, it's a done deal.

The supreme payoff of self-discipline is that when you make a conscious decision to do something and know before you

> Procrastination and indulgence are nothing more than creditors who charge us interest.

begin that success is virtually guaranteed, you'll follow through on that decision. You will explode the common misconception that self-discipline is hard because it's only hard for a short time. Yet it's the things that seem easy in the short term that become harder in the long run because procrastination and indulgence are nothing more than creditors who charge us interest.

Self-discipline can empower you to overcome any addiction or lose any amount of weight. It can wipe out procrastination, disorder, distraction, and ignorance. It can change the course of your career, the path of your financial future, and the trajectory of the rest of your life.

That's what *Take the Stairs* is all about—making better decisions in order to improve your self-discipline and your life. A Take the Stairs mind-set can be your first step to liberating your potential, and it is the pathway to achieving anything your heart desires.

Of all qualities, self-discipline is one special quality that will guarantee you greater successes, bigger accomplishments, and more fulfilling happiness. Of a thousand principles for success developed over the ages, this one quality or practice will do more to assure that you accomplish wonderful things with your life than any other.

Self-discipline is a habit, a practice, a philosophy, and a way of living. Taking the stairs is a mind-set; but it's not even about the stairs. You might not physically be able to take the silly stairs—but *anyone* can start making more disciplined choices.

However, self-discipline is diminishing in our modern culture. Our friends, families, and companies are losing to distraction, temptation, creative avoidance, indulgence, apathy, and procrastination because we have been conditioned to believe that we deserve immediate satisfaction and that the government or some other entity will bail us out whenever we need it.

We've become soft, overweight, and spoiled. Sadly, at least in America, we have become a ProcrastiNation.

The Hidden Cost of the "Easy Way"

A study of 10,000 U.S. employees indicated that the average worker self-admitted to wasting 2.09 hours each day on non-job-related activities. Considering the average salaried employee makes $39,795, that means procrastination costs employers $10,396 per year per employee!

If you work for a small company of about 100 employees, then as much as $1 million a year could be lost in productivity because of procrastination. The scariest part is that the problem is so pervasive it's almost completely imperceptible. The same is true in our lives!

Since most of us aren't making disciplined choices, it becomes increasingly difficult to notice ourselves doing things that are self-defeating. It's hard to take notice of $5,000 of debt when you hear about people going bankrupt for overspending by hundreds of thousands. My 10 pounds of fat isn't as salient when I'm standing next to people who are 30 pounds overweight. And why shouldn't I get a divorce if 50% of the people around me are doing the same thing?

It seems like many of us have fallen asleep to problems that are *directly within our control.* Often we don't even pay attention to them because we're too consumed with our iPod, our email, or our text messages. These distractions soothe us in the moment, but in the bigger picture they only compound the problem. As it turns out, distraction is a dangerously deceptive saboteur of our goals.

Think about it. Haven't you noticed that the gym is empty and the food court is packed? Do most people around you pay with cash, or pull out a credit card? Are TV shows celebrating commitment, discipline, and hard work, or are they touting temptation, drama, and greed? To be honest, I didn't really notice it either . . . until one day I looked at a vacant set of stairs and a jam-packed escalator.

> Distraction is a dangerously deceptive saboteur of our goals.

Until we acknowledge this damaging trend, we won't stop looking for shortcuts. There are seldom any true shortcuts. Usually there are just deluding self-serving short-term facades. And many of us are buying into them.

The popular book and movie *The Secret* teaches us that we create our lives with every thought of every minute of every day. Yes, this is true and I believe in the concept and practice it every day—but if we don't get off our butts and take action, we won't achieve anything. The real secret to success has more to do with *action* than *attraction*. We just don't talk about it as much because it doesn't sell as well.

The 4-Hour Workweek, the bestselling book written by Timothy Ferriss, promotes a lifestyle that sounds like fun except the part we missed is that it is available only to those who first work their tail off in order to be able to set it up that way. Again, I subscribe to the concepts and have gotten a lot of mileage from the author's fascinating body of work. Yet at the same time I have yet to meet a single successful person who didn't achieve their dream lifestyle without paying a price, without sacrifice, without self-discipline—including what I know about the impressive Tim Ferriss himself.

Ask an Olympic athlete. Read Michael Jordan's autobiography. Listen to what Peyton Manning says is his secret. They all attribute their successes more to having the self-discipline to work harder and push farther in practice than to an innate talent. Sure, people who achieve greatness in any endeavor might be blessed with some natural talent; and sure, timing and luck play a part. But as Malcolm Gladwell demonstrated in his book *Outliers*, there's no substitute for hard work—10,000 hours of it, to be exact!

Don't you have certain natural talents? Aren't there some passions you were born with? Of course. The question is: Are you using them?

Most of us would agree—at least on a joking level—that we could use more self-discipline. We often know what we *should* do and we even have some intentions of *doing* those things, but we never really get around to it. It's not because we're bad people, or that other people have more talents, opportunities, or gifts than we do; it's just because nobody ever taught us how to think about hard work. This book will. This book won't just increase your motivation; it will shift your mind-set.

After reading this book, you'll know what separates top performers from average performers. You'll understand how your mind-set makes it so difficult to work out, get ahead, or make a difference. You'll even understand why your well-intentioned New Year's Resolutions never materialize.

So why don't we do those things that we know we should do? Maybe it's because things are moving so fast. We're all running a million miles per hour, going a thousand different directions. And in the noise of distraction it's so easy for time to pass by without our realizing it.

Our unwillingness to take action in our own individual lives might not seem like a global problem. But as our procrastination ripples through our homes, our schools, our communities, and our culture at large, we find our country becoming a ProcrastiNation unwilling to take on the tough challenges we face, and seeking immediate gratification instead of real growth and change.

This book is not about solving the world's problems, but it is about helping you overcome your own challenges. It's a book about helping you do the things you've thought about, talked about, and dreamt about. You are in charge of your finances. You are in control of how you look. You have the power within you to live your dreams. You are in charge of your thinking. You are responsible for your results. It is time to throw off that cloak of apathy, to let go of the desire to blame, and to begin being willing to commit to making a meaningful change in your behavior.

As with many great lessons in life, I first learned about committing to the ridiculous from my early mistakes.

Commit to the Ridiculous

When I was a young boy, I had a problem with remembering to lock the door. It seemed that about once a week, I would leave the house for Lafayette Elementary School without remembering to lock our front door. Since I was being raised by a single mother who went to work early in the mornings and my older brother, Randy, left a few hours before I did, it was up to me to make sure the house was locked each morning.

My mom first discovered my sluggish habit of forgetting to

lock the door when she would come home from work for lunch every now and again, only to find the door unlocked. Plus, my brother would come home from school about a half hour before me each day and would occasionally find that I had forgotten to lock the door.

Both my brother and my mother sat down with me on repeated occasions and tried to explain to me the importance of locking the door and how dangerous it was to leave the house wide open. Each time, I swore to them that I understood why it was important and that they could count on me to remember from then on. But for whatever reason, I would start off strong and then eventually I would slip back into forgetting to lock the door—a habit that will be familiar to anyone who has ever abandoned a New Year's Resolution . . . more later on why this happens.

And then it happened. One day, I was the last to leave the house, and after school, my brother went to a friend's, which meant that I was the first one home. I'll never forget the fear that gripped my heart like a vise when I walked up to the house only to find the front door was wide open. As I crept into the living room, I noticed it had been completely ransacked! The couch was flipped, pillows were everywhere, and the TV was missing! Salty tears began trickling down my face.

Thoughts began racing through my mind. "Had I locked the door?" "What happened?" "Is someone still in the house?" "This is all my fault!" "Mom is going to be so mad at me." "Is there some other explanation?"

Without being totally sure of what happened, I slowly tip-toed around the corner into my room. TV, VCR, Nintendo, stereo—all gone! We'd been robbed! I dropped my bag, and sprinted out the door! My heart was pounding, tears streaming, and knees trembling. I ran to a neighbor's house and called my mother.

A few moments later, my mom's car pulled up in the driveway. I remember the awkward feelings of safety juxtaposed with the intense fear of the ramifications I knew were coming.

When my mom pulled up, I ran out of the house and into her arms, crying, "I'm sorry, I'm sorry. I'm so sorry, Mom." On my mom's face was a warm but unusual smile. And about that moment, behind my mom's car, a truck pulled in. It was loaded with furniture and electronics. At that moment, I realized who had robbed our house—my mother!

I continued crying, this time with frustration and anger mixed with a certain relief that we had been robbed on her lunch break by Mom. Once I calmed down, she explained to me why she had done what she had done: to teach me a lesson, to show me for my own good and for our family's good the importance of locking the door.

After having felt the "consequences" of my actions, I can honestly say that I've never left my house or anyone else's house in my life without double- and triple-checking to make sure the door was locked. Although the experience was painful, it did work. My mom was willing to go to the level of the *ridiculous* so that I would learn the lesson. Are you? How committed are

> How committed are you to changing your life for the better? What are you willing to sacrifice?

you to changing your life for the better? What are you willing to sacrifice?

For where we are in our lives, for the way things are happening in our world, and for what it's going to take to make things better—we have to be willing to go to the level of the ridiculous. Which is why I decided awhile back to start taking the stairs everywhere instead of taking the escalator. It's a symbolic gesture, but people all around me have noticed it; they understand the reason behind this everyday practice, and they, too, have committed to start to Take the Stairs as an outward sign of their inner commitment to lead a more self-disciplined life.

While I initially learned about self-discipline in martial arts and in my family life, there is no doubt that I honed it the most when I worked as a salesperson for the Southwestern Company. For the last 150 years, Southwestern has become famous for "building character in young people" by training college-aged students to run their own business. During this summer program, these students sell children's educational materials known as the Southwestern Advantage from door to door.

Each summer in college I would leave my tiny hometown of Frederick, Colorado, and travel to Nashville, Tennessee, for an intensive week of sales training, and then I'd go to a city away from home and work fourteen hours a day, six days a week, on straight profit. Since 1855 and still to this day, about 3,000 students do this every summer in the Southwestern program with the goal of transforming the way students learn at home by giving them access to a proprietary system for proven success. Without a doubt, it is one of the toughest and most rigorous yet enriching programs a young person can participate in.

What's amazing is that the average first-year dealer in the program who finishes the summer makes a gross profit of around $8,500, with the top students in the program usually earning profits of well over $50,000 in one summer. Two of my business partners today, Dustin Hillis and Dave Brown, both broke the company record one summer while in college, earning close to $100,000 each between May and August!

Although I had a fairly successful selling career, earning more than $250,000 during my college summers, I was commonly known as the guy who recruited small armies of people to go door-to-door each year because I had recruited fifty-seven students to work in the program over a three-year period.

What's interesting is that a lot of people don't realize how much I struggled.

It was about 2:30 in the afternoon on my second day of my very first summer, and it had been raining all morning. I hadn't been in a door since 8:15 a.m. and I had yet to sell anything. A guy had just screamed at me to get off his porch, and it sent me into a tailspin to where a short while later I had gotten myself completely lost.

The rain had basically dissolved my map, I was shivering

from the cold, and the blisters on my prune-wrinkled feet were slowing me down. Confused as to where I was, emotionally spent, and feeling desolate, I sat down on a curb. I'll never forget looking down at my handwritten map and seeing the words "Buckingham Lane" and "Coral Court" merge together by a stream of my running tears.

How did I end up here? Why am I sitting on a curb in Montgomery, Alabama? What was I thinking to get myself into this? Is this really happening to me right now? How am I ever going to survive ninety more days of this?

Here I was an accounting major who took this job because I thought if I could learn how to sell, maybe I could have money—which I had never had before. Yet I seemed to have only made things worse as now I was apart from any family, any friends, and it seemed at the moment that not a single person in this neighborhood wanted me here.

I had been stripped of all my self-confidence and now I was failing all on my own. I felt that no one saw, no one knew, and no one cared. As I was sitting on the curb, I realized that I resented my job, I wanted to quit, and I wanted to go home.

For you, in your life or your business, have you ever had a moment like that? Where you couldn't believe how bad things were going and you couldn't see a way out? Maybe it wasn't with a job but maybe it was some relationship struggle? Or possibly you were in a battle for your health? Or perhaps you were dealing with some major financial concern?

Whatever it was for you, I firmly believe that all of us, sooner or later, will end up having one of these curbside moments. The surroundings and circumstances will be different, but the feelings will be the same. And although we will all be able to find justifications for why we can quit, give up, or pass blame, the truth is at the end of the day we have to live with the choices we make in these critical moments. Are we going to give up, or are we going to be the kind of people who stand up and do what it takes, even if we don't feel like doing it?

> Are we going to give up, or are we going to be the kind of people who stand up and do what it takes, even if we don't feel like doing it?

Although it was incredibly challenging and I thought about quitting on several occasions, I went back summer after summer. Today, people sometimes ask me why I kept going back, and I have a very simple answer. While it was a difficult job and I never liked going door-to-door, I loved the philosophies the company was teaching me. I loved the people I was working with. Most of all, I loved the person that I was becoming in the process. It was making me stronger, smarter, and more self-aware. I'm eternally grateful I had that opportunity to learn those lessons as a student working under the supervision of strong leadership.

Life isn't fair. Life isn't easy. Being successful doesn't happen by falling into the most desirable situation possible and somehow magically being discovered for some special uniqueness we have that no one else does. That's an unfortunate fairy tale that many of us live by. The truth is that success comes from being tested in the fire, being pushed to your limits, and having your character and confidence shaped by challenging circumstances. Successful people view problems and challenges as setbacks or hindrances, but they know that the more challenges they have, the higher the likelihood that they will develop the character required to become great.

> Do we have what it takes to do the things we know are good for us even when we don't feel like doing them?

I discovered later that many people of notable success in life, including three state governors, U.S. senators and congressman, CEOs and founders of major companies, presidents of universities, and founders of major not-for-profit organizations attribute much of their success to having sold with Southwestern while in college. They, too, had their share of curbside moments but chose not to quit.

Simply stated, there are only two types of activities: things we feel like doing and things we don't. And if we can learn to make ourselves do the things we don't want to do, then we have literally created the power to create any result in our lives.

It's pretty safe to assume that we will always continue doing the things that we want to do. So then the only real question is: Do we have what it takes to do the things we know are good for us even when we don't feel like doing them?

That is one of the only things that separates people who get what they want out of life from those who don't. If that was the only skill you needed to learn in order to have everything you wanted, could you do it?

Small Choices Yield Big Results

If we take an escalator, then there is literally no physical change in our bodies once we're at the top because all we do is stand there while a machine does all the work. However, when we Take the Stairs, a number of things happen, if only to a minor extent. We burn calories, we use (tear) our muscles, and our heart rate increases as we climb. So, there are physiological changes that take place when we Take the Stairs as opposed to taking the escalator. The same is true in your life!

While climbing one set of stairs might not be enough to make a noticeable difference in your health, it certainly could make a difference if it became your daily habit. That's why author Albert Gray once said, "Successful people form the habit of doing things that failures don't like doing."

It's the *habit* that's important. Success is often not the result of our major decisions, but more deceptively it is the aggregate sum total of all our small and seemingly insignificant ones. Success comes down to choosing the hard right over the easy wrong. Consistently.

What if we did adopt the habit to Take the Stairs in both a literal and metaphorical sense? Imagine how simple that would make our decisions. Whenever we had a choice to make, we would choose the "hard right" over the "easy wrong." We could make decisions quickly and with confidence knowing that most people will not make the same choices that we make, but also trusting that most people will not have the same development, growth, or results that we have. Those are exactly the choices that successful people are making all over the planet right now!

The Myth of the Invisible Finish Line

Most of us live our lives chasing after an invisible finish line. We are constantly in search of the next destination, living under the falsehood that something awaits us there that will give us a sense of fulfillment we currently don't have.

We say things like:

- Once I finish college, I'll make the money I need.
- If I could just find the right person to marry, I know I'd be happy.
- Once the kids leave the house . . .
- After I get that promotion . . .
- When I retire . . .

Of course, some of those things do happen, but the *feelings* we seek never actually last. Because in our never-ending search for the next destination, we miss out on one of life's great truths, which is, just as the legendary philosopher Hannah Montana said, "It's all about the climb."

When I interview some of the most successful people on the planet, they consistently talk about a mind-set that pushes toward a destination—but more than that, one that embraces the path and one that finds joy in the journey. Their mentality is altogether different. While most people seem to complain and rant about life's challenges, these ultrasuccessful people, some of which you'll meet in this book, seem to learn how to fall in love with the daily grind.

Successful people take pride in tackling the tasks that other

> Learn to fall in love with the daily grind.

people rebuke. They understand that there is no real finish line, no magic moment when they will "arrive" and get to rest on their laurels. Discipline is a perpetual process, and the growth is in the journey. Simple, but here's the part that you won't like hearing—you don't get a day off. Ever.

Before you close this book and throw it across the room, there's good news. Just because you don't get a day off doesn't mean you're going to be miserable. Quite the contrary. The purpose of a Take the Stairs mind-set is to set you up with a life that you can't wait to live every day. There will be pain on the front end, but once you have formed the habits of self-discipline in every area of your life, you won't *want* a day off. You will have a life that you love and it won't be temporary; it will be permanent.

The Rent Axiom

The reason you have to commit to being disciplined every day for the rest of your life is because of something we at Southwestern call the Rent Axiom, which states that success is never owned, it is only rented—and the rent is due every day.

Of course, everyone has their own definition of what success is. The Rent Axiom allows for that.

Maybe you want a healthy body, or a thriving business, or

financial security, or a happy marriage. Substitute those things for success above, and you'll see what I mean that all of them are "rented."

> Success is never owned, it is only rented, and the rent is due every day.

No matter where you are at on the spectrum of discipline, you can improve and grow. Likewise, no matter where you are, you also have some parts figured out. The process you're about to undertake will build a foundation for which a disciplined life can flourish. This process is going to change the rest of your life. You are now becoming the person you've always wanted to be.

You may feel like you are getting ready for an uphill battle, and you probably are. Yet the rewards on the other side of this transformation are endless because you are creating the power and freedom to do anything in your life.

So while this may not seem "fun," it is only that way for a while. Once you get used to taking the stairs, you will find that it's exhilarating, freeing, and invigorating. Plus, with this new-found power in your life, you will be able to design it any way you want it. Remember that once you love what you do, then you never have to work a day in your life.

Seven Strategies for Self-Discipline

In the chapters that follow, I will introduce you to the seven strategies you'll need in order to Take the Stairs to the life you've always wanted. They are seven principles that you can count on that are reflected in the minds and lives of the people I've met, seen, read, or talked to who are living their dreams.

I didn't sit in a room and think these concepts up. In fact, I'm nothing more than a conduit of information that has been assimilated from a variety of sources. What you're about to learn are truths that I've gleaned from successful people around the world. What I'm sharing are not all my ideas but evidence of what I learned from all of them. They worked for them, they worked for me, and they will work for you.

The seven principles for simplifying self-discipline to liberate your potential are:

1. Sacrifice: The Paradox Principle
2. Commitment: The Buy-In Principle
3. Focus: The Magnification Principle
4. Integrity: The Creation Principle
5. Schedule: The Harvest Principle
6. Faith: The Perspective Principle
7. Action: The Pendulum Principle

Each strategy is built around a central framework or concept for that chapter, and each concludes with a simple straightforward strategy that can be implemented right away. There is an action item at the end of each chapter to help get you started on implementing more self-discipline in your life. This includes a few exclusive links that are *only* listed in this book that take you to hidden pages with video lessons, an exercise, and a personal action plan that goes along with some of the chapters. Additionally, if you go to www.takethestairsbook.com/focused40, you can take a quiz that will help you rate your current level of self-discipline in comparison to many of the people who were studied for this book. Both the test and the score with recommendations are free.

Self-discipline is the simplest and fastest way to make life as easy as possible. It is the key to everything you've ever dreamed of. Discipline creates freedom—the freedom to do anything! It is what took me from being a poor Hispanic boy raised by a single mother in a trailer park to speaking in front of thousands of people in just a few short years.

Are you ready to start this journey?

Your time is now.

For daily reminders about building discipline, find Rory on Facebook at www.roryonfacebook.com.

1

SACRIFICE

THE PARADOX PRINCIPLE

n our quest for self-discipline, we would all be wise to adopt a buffalo mentality. Yes, buffalo. Let me explain.

I proudly grew up in central Colorado. When I was young, my mom, my brother, and I lived in trailer parks and apartments all around Boulder, Lafayette, and Louisville. When people think about Colorado, they often think about the world-famous Rocky Mountains all over the western part of the state. What they often forget is that we also have the great Kansas plains that roll from the foothills out toward the east. Because of that unique topographical landscape, we are one of the only places in the world that has both buffalo and cows.

One of my favorite places that I look to for principles of

success and the way the world works is in nature. The way these two creatures, buffalo and cows, respond in nature has some really powerful lessons for us.

When a storm approaches from the west, as storms almost always do out there, cows respond in a very predictable way. They know the storm is coming from the west, so they head east to try to outrun the storm.

The only problem is that, as you may know, cows are not real fast. Before long, the storm catches up to them—and the cows, not knowing any better, keep on running. Instead of outrunning the storm, they actually run *with* the storm, maximizing their exposure to it. Isn't that stupid?

Many of us humans do the same thing every day.

We try to avoid conflict that is inevitable. So often, whether it's in our relationship disputes, financial troubles, or even our physical health, we try to "ignore" problems, pretending that they aren't that big of a deal, and then we try to run away at the last minute as they're fast approaching. Unfortunately, as most of us have learned the hard way, problems tend to compound when we ignore them, and we end up being exposed to something worse than what it might have been.

What buffalo do, on the other hand, is truly unique. They wait for the storm to cross right over the crest of the peak of the mountaintop, and as it arrives, they turn and charge directly into the storm. By running at the storm, they run straight through it as the storm passes overhead, which minimizes the amount of pain they experience.

If only more of us would tackle life's inevitable, unavoidable problems the way the buffalo do—head-on. Problems that are procrastinated on are only amplified, and we're the ones who pay the price. There's a great deal of strength—and strategic payoff—in charging at our most challenging circumstances head-on. But for us, unlike for the buffalo, it's a skill we have to learn, practice, and maintain.

> Problems that are procrastinated on are only amplified, and we're the ones who pay the price.

The Pain Paradox

Let's say you're sitting on the couch. It's Tuesday night, and you're trying to decide, "Should I go to the gym?" or "Should I relax and stay at home and watch TV?" We're faced with these types of decisions all the time:

"Should I go ahead and buy that item or just save my money for a rainy day?"

"Should I have that extravagant dessert or call it quits for the night?"

"Should I put in the extra effort here or just get by with the minimum amount required?"

While there are thousands of scenarios like this in our lives, the process for deciding is basically always the same.

In making any decision, there are two opposing sets of criteria that typically influence our choices. One part of our brain is processing our emotions and impulses, encouraging us to make the choice based on what feels good. But there is another part of our brain that is analytical. It is evaluating what is rational, and quietly asking us to consider what makes sense logically. These two forces are in a constant tug-of-war, pulling us back and forth in opposite directions.

We know, rationally speaking, what we should do, but we also feel, emotionally speaking, what we'd like to do. Our human tendency is to make the decision based on the force that is most substantial right here and now. And in the short term, our emotions, feelings, and impulses almost always outweigh the logical considerations—which is why the vast majority of people make decisions based on emotions and impulses.

Most of us make decisions this way because we want our life to be easy, and doing whatever makes us feel good is easy in the short term. However, these choices that

> Choices that are easy in the short term are very often in direct conflict with what makes life easy in the long term.

are easy in the short term are very often in direct conflict with what makes life easy in the long term.

For example, drugs and other substances can make us feel great in the short term, but they lead to a whole string of negative emotional, physical, and financial consequences in the long term. Marital unfaithfulness can satisfy a short-term desire but often destroys families. Even something as small as neglecting physical exercise spares us from working out in the short term, but quickly catches up with us in medical expenses, decreased energy, and low self-esteem in the long term. The great irony here is that what seems easy and feels good in the short term usually doesn't last long.

Successful people know that making decisions based on what feels good in the short term is often a deceiving shortcut that requires more work in the end. Similarly, they know that creating an easy life in the long term requires choosing some challenging activities here and now. For example, the nature of becoming wealthy requires that rather than spending our money we save it or invest it. Living a longer, healthier life might demand that we disallow the excess of certain types of foods and other substances into our body. Advancing to an influential role in an organization or in our career most likely requires more education, tougher projects, and stricter deadlines.

So, counterintuitively an easy life in the long term comes from the sacrifice of completing more difficult tasks here and now. But the paradigm-shifting insight and breakthrough that successful people have made that many others have not is that *often these more difficult activities are only necessary for a short amount of time.*

Which brings us to the Pain Paradox of decision making that states the short-term easy leads to the long-term difficult, while the short-term difficult leads to the long-term easy. The great paradox is that what we thought was the easy way, what looks like the easy way, what seems like the easy way very often leads us to creating a life that couldn't be more opposite of easy. And inversely the things that we thought were most difficult, the challenges that appear to be the toughest, and the requirements that seem most rigorous are the very activities that lead us to the life of easy that we all want.

Therefore, it's not that successful people are somehow born with a mysterious predisposition for success that the rest of us don't have. It's that the criteria successful people use to process decisions is altogether different. Successful people know that feelings and impulses don't tend to last long; they are short term. So while most people make decisions based on the short-term emotion, successful people can make sacrifices because they base their decisions on long-term logic. Yet the subtle difference in how they make decisions yields tremendously improved results over the course of their lives.

What seems easy in the short term really isn't easy in the long term.

It's an empowering realization to understand that successful people have the very same impulses and the very same "emotional pulls," and that they often feel inclined to make the same decisions as everyone else. But they know (either instinctively or because they've disciplined themselves) that in the long term it is the logical considerations that matter most.

What seems easy in the short term really isn't easy in the long term. What seems hard isn't hard for very long. But we spend so much of our lives trying to make things easier and avoiding things that are difficult in the short term without realizing that much of the time it is that very behavior that makes things worse in the long term. Understanding and embracing the Pain Paradox is one of the most important things you can do on your path to true success.

Every day we are faced with thousands of choices, all of which must be filtered through this exact same decision-making process. The Pain Paradox fundamentally demonstrates why success, and becoming a successful person, is more a matter of choice than of circumstance. It is as straightforward as choosing between left or right, up or down, black or white.

Surprisingly, success in life rarely comes from making big, grandiose decisions. Rather, success is the aggregate sum total of small, seemingly insignificant choices that when compounded over time create the trajectory of our lives. As it turns out, success really is as simple as choosing between taking the escalator and taking the stairs.

> Success is more a matter of choice than of circumstance.

Which Would You Prefer?

You probably have a credit card in your pocket, so imagine what it would be like if you drove to the mall right now and went on a big spending spree. Wouldn't that feel good for a while?

In the short term, you'd get to live it up like a rock star and you could get whatever you wanted. And chances are you'd have a blast!

Seem unrealistic? Did you know that in the United States, 1 out of every 9 twelve-year-olds is carrying a credit card? Did you know that 18 million college students in the United States have credit cards, and that according to Sallie Mae, 82% of them don't pay off their card balances each month?

If we go have a carelessly good time at the mall, does that create easy long-term consequences or difficult long-term consequences?

On the other hand, if we decided to skip the shopping spree, stick to a monthly budget, and save more than we spend, we'd be accumulating resources for when we really need them. We'd be "buying" ourselves more freedom in the long term.

The Paradox Principle of Sacrifice applies to virtually every area of our life, and will be familiar to anyone who's ever been on a diet, tried to get into better shape, or attempted to improve their financial health. Yet far too often we push aside what we already know, and act on our short-term desires, only to pay a much bigger price in the long run.

LONG-TERM PAYS BETTER

Case Study: Jeff Dobyns, Financial Services, Nashville, Tennessee

There are a lot of financial planners in the world, and sometimes it's hard to distinguish one from the next. One advisor named Jeff Dobyns decided to take a long-term approach, and has ended up becoming very successful in a short period of time, building the number one producing office globally for Raymond James, out of 1,200 branches worldwide. And in an industry dominated by people with more than 30 years of experience, it's quite impressive that Jeff has accomplished this in only 13.

As with many ultraperformers, Jeff is a bit perplexed when asked what he does that is *special*, because in his mind, it isn't. He says:

It's always made so much sense to me that you have to pay a price up front for the rewards that come later on. The first five to ten years of this business take a lot of sacrifice to make the business run the right way. Unfortunately, we sometimes see young people wanting to focus more on balance than putting in the work, and it inevitably prolongs the time until their desired freedom comes. Going "all in" to any endeavor is the best way to be free of mental clutter that stifles our progress. It's the fastest way to get us where we want to go.

Also, it's not just about working hard, but also making sacrifices to do the right thing. There are countless times when I've given clients advice that forfeits me commissions in the short term because another vehicle is honestly the best strategy for them. That type of advice could've gotten me fired in some organizations, yet it has become the very foundation that our reputation is built on.

Over time, you develop a strong faith and realize that if you do the right things, everything will work out. But it's always an ongoing process, because as we master the process of sacrifice in one area of our life or business, it seems like we're often just beginning to practice it in another.

But in every area of life, those sacrifices become easier and easier to make, until one day they become automatic. It's a surprising revelation that what started as a disciplined sacrifice later becomes a deep source of satisfaction. We take pride in putting in the work necessary and making it a priority to do the right things for clients. What I think most people underestimate is how much greater the impacts are—positive or negative—in the long term.

The Compound Effect

We often underestimate the invisible compounding effect that accentuates the impacts of our choices. Earlier I mentioned that procrastination costs the average company $10,396 per year per employee. Obviously, that's a lot of money, but what is that amount worth over a long period of time?

Hypothetically let's imagine that a company took that $10,396 per year and, rather than spending it on a procrastinating employee, invested it into the stock market.

Historically a good growth stock mutual fund grows at an average rate of around 12%. So let's pretend that a company invested the money from just one employee into a mutual fund for a period of 30 years. What do you think that one person's procrastination would be worth to that company? A total of $311,000. For just one employee!

You might say, "That's too bad for companies," and you're right, but what about the price the employee himself faces, in the form of missed opportunities, lack of progress, and the sinking feeling of not having met his full potential? What about all of the small businesses in the world that run on a shoestring budget? Or how about all of the salespeople who are paid on commission—or anyone paid for their results, for that matter?

In many cases, this money is real and it's coming right out of our own pockets. It's money that we could be investing to build wealth, and we don't even talk about it because it doesn't show up in our checkbook register or on our income statements. Unfortunately we don't appropriately value things we don't directly pay for. Yet it turns out that procrastination is one of the most expensive invisible costs in business today.

In his book *The Compound*

> Procrastination is one of the most expensive invisible costs in business today.

Effect, author Darren Hardy explains how this dynamic touches every area of our life. "Every dollar you spend today is worth at least $5 in 20 years and $10 in 30 years (assuming only 8% growth rate)." So that $5 a day coffee is really taking $25 out of your future pocket.

The good news is that it works in a positive direction, too. For example, a one-time investment of $1,000 at an 8% return for 40 years is worth just under $22,000!

These numbers demonstrate and quantify the forces at play related to the Paradox Principle of Sacrifice, but they don't even come close to properly accounting for the enormous costs that affect unquantifiable areas of our lives.

That phone call or apology you know you should make to a friend or family member that you haven't—how much is that costing you?

Or how about your physical health issues that you keep ignoring and writing off as no big deal—guess what, my friend, they're going to cost you exponentially more in the future, guaranteed.

What about this one . . . remember that dream you've had your entire life that you've never taken action on? You tell me, how much is that weighing on your sense of freedom and peace of mind?

All of these things are robbing you of the joy you deserve to have in your life. All of them are retrievable with enough self-discipline and by employing the Paradox Principle of Sacrifice.

It starts by realizing that a sacrifice isn't really a sacrifice at all; it's just a short-term down payment on a rich future blessing.

Gifts Come in Mysterious Ways

As a child, I loved the Volume Library. The Volume Library was a set of reference books that my mom bought for me (interestingly, purchased from a Southwestern student dealer who had knocked on our door) that helped me with forty different school subjects. And I loved it growing up because it had math and science, and naked people!

But what does it really mean to sacrifice? If I give you $1, is that a sacrifice? What if Bill Gates gives you $1, is that really a sacrifice?

My mom used to tell me, "Rory, gifts come in mysterious ways." As I mentioned, I was raised by a single mother, and my mom happened to sell Mary Kay cosmetics. Which means that growing up I was surrounded by women who were constantly teaching me all the principles of success—it also means that I know more about makeup than I do about cars.

As fate would have it, when I grew up and went to college and started selling with Southwestern, I was selling that very same set of books—the Volume Library.

My first summer was in Montgomery, Alabama, and I remember pulling up to this one house that sat way back off the road behind several other houses.

As I knocked on the door, a frail single mother answered, and standing next to her was the cutest five-year-old boy. He had dirt on his face and he spoke with a little bit of a lisp, but he was smiling from ear to ear. The little boy wanted the books so badly, but there was no way this family could afford the $300 cost.

His mom practically begged me to give them the summer to save up and asked me to come back at the end of the summer because she was trying to show her kids that education is the fastest way out of poverty.

I had a soft spot in my heart for this kid and so I said, "I'll tell you what, little buddy, I promise to save you a set of books and to come back at the end of the summer if *you* promise to save up all of your money for me in this little envelope and have it waiting at the end of the summer when I return."

Excitedly he agreed.

The summer went by and I had honestly forgotten about the family until it came time to deliver their books. As I pulled up to their house, I saw the whole scene again and I almost just kept driving because there was no way this family was going to have the money.

But I had made a promise to the little boy so I dragged myself out of the car and went up to the house and from inside I heard him, "Mom! It's Mr. Bookman! He came back!"

He ran outside and grabbed me by the arm and pulled me

into the house, where his mom was on the couch in a hospital gown, and instantly I knew things had gone from bad to worse.

The little boy's smile suddenly turned to tears as he came up to me with the envelope in his hand. "I had it for you, Mr. Bookman. I had all of it, but Mommy needed help."

It turned out that, with the help of his nine-year-old sister, this little boy had mowed lawns, had sold lemonade, and had even sold some of his baseball cards, and he'd saved up every single dollar for those books, but then his mom got sick and you know the rest of the story . . .

I didn't know what to do as I was only eighteen years old at the time so I just gave him the biggest hug and then left. As I drove around the block, I thought about the lesson that I had just learned from a five-year-old. It's a lesson they don't teach much in schools anymore, and you can't read about it in the Volume Library.

So I did what you would do; I did what anyone would've done. I went back to that house and left an extra set of books on the porch with a sticky note that said, "Gifts Come in Mysterious Ways."

That little boy taught me about the secret of sacrifice: It's the person who makes the sacrifice that gets the gift—sometimes in ways we wouldn't have expected.

Create a clear picture of what you want in the long run and you will find that your endurance for pain and strife, discipline and hard work will naturally increase to levels you never thought you had. A new world will open up for you—a world where you can have anything you want . . . as long as you commit.

To see videos corresponding to this chapter, visit www .takethestairsbook.com/paradoxprinciple.

2
COMMITMENT

THE BUY-IN PRINCIPLE

A man named Bob is in a restroom, standing in front of a urinal—and he is suddenly in a bit of a predicament. Somehow he's managed to drop a $5 bill into the urinal. Just as Bob is looking down thinking about what he's going to do, another gentleman named Dave happens to walk into the restroom.

Dave sees the $5 in the urinal, assesses the situation with an empathetic sigh, and then says, "Oh, that's a tough decision. What are you going to do?"

Bob thinks about it for a moment. Looks at the urinal, and then looks back at Dave. A split second later Bob pulls out his wallet, and out of nowhere grabs a $50 bill and *throws it into the urinal*!

In shock, Dave exclaims, "Man, what are you doing? I can't

believe you just did that. That's fifty dollars!" Bob looks back at Dave, cracks a smile, and replies, "Well, c'mon, you don't think I'd stick my hand in there for just five dollars, do you?"

This is an old story, but it illustrates something that is critical in your ability to be more self-disciplined. I call it the Buy-In Principle of Commitment, and it simply states that the more we have invested in something, the less likely we are to let it fail.

> The more we have invested in something, the less likely we are to let it fail.

Have you ever known people who seem to have so much potential but are never able to put it together to become a top performer? Have you ever wondered why so many well-intentioned couples end up getting a divorce? Ever been curious why some people accept accountability for their choices while others seem always to be victims of their circumstances?

The answer to all of those questions is found in the way we make decisions at life's critical pivot points.

The Commitment Continuum

No matter how you define success, getting there will inevitably require that you expend energy—physical energy, sure—but also emotional energy, which is seldom discussed but often the reason so many of us give up on our most meaningful endeavors.

As the chart below illustrates, emotional commitment intensifies as we pursue any activity. It starts out easy, and gets more challenging, culminating in a peak, or a "pivot point."

That key moment usually shows up in our life as some sort of breakdown. It's when we're faced with the decision to keep going or to turn back. It is that key moment you hear successful people talk about as the moment everything fell apart and they had a choice to make—which, looking back later, they realized was the turning point in their life.

We are all going to face that pivot point hundreds, if not thousands, of times in various areas of our lives. Some people never seem to push through those points, while others do. Everyone— whether we are successful or not—faces these critical pivot points, and more important, we all yearn to move quickly past the point of emotional turmoil and uncertainty, to return to a state of normalcy and calm. But it's how we think in these critical moments that makes all the difference.

It's interesting to note that very often the emotional energy of making a decision is greater than the physical energy of executing that decision. In other words, it's not

> Very often the emotional energy of making a decision is greater than the physical energy of executing that decision.

THE COMMITMENT CONTINUUM

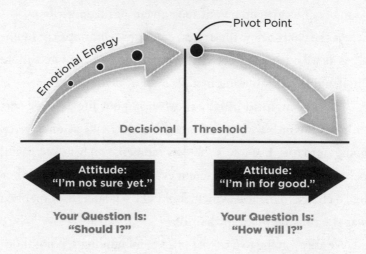

Pivot Point

Emotional Energy

Decisional | Threshold

Attitude:
"I'm not sure yet."

Attitude:
"I'm in for good."

Your Question Is:
"Should I?"

Your Question Is:
"How will I?"

working out once we get to the gym that is hard; it's sitting on the couch deciding whether or not we're going to go that is more difficult and therefore more important. Both successful people and average people struggle with all different types of tough choices and pivot points. And even though the methodology they use for making their decisions is only slightly varied, it creates substantial long-term differences. It comes down to nothing more than a one-degree change in their attitude.

Turning Back

Things get difficult for all of us, but the people who turn back approach the endeavor with an attitude that is usually along the lines of "I'm not so sure about this yet." "I'm not sure this is the right job." "I'm not sure that they're the right person." "I'm not sure I have the right skills." "I'm not sure this is the right time."

Because of that doubt, they plague themselves with the question "Should I?" "Should I keep going?" "Should I try to make this work?" "Should I look at something else?" "Should I leave this person?" "Should I get a new job?" They run around asking "should, should, should" so much that they turn into what I like to call a "should-head."

That seemingly harmless mind-set of "I'm not sure" and "Should I?" is just enough at the critical pivot point to swing our commitment back in the opposite direction. We go in the opposite direction because we *know* we can return our emotional energy expenditure to normal if we go back to where we come from or if we move on to something new.

The problem with this approach is that the perfect situation never comes! There will never be a perfect time, there will never be a perfect person, there will never be a perfect situation to start doing the things we need to get us where we want to go. We need to stop spending so much of our time trying to make the *right*

> We need to stop spending so much of our time trying to make the *right* decisions and instead start spending our time making decisions and then *making them* right.

decisions and instead start spending our time making decisions and then *making them* right.

When we abandon the challenge at hand and instead get on with whatever the new thing is—a new job, a new relationship, a new exercise plan, a new gadget, a new city or town—we start the entire process over but almost always end up right back in the same place. That happens because we are incognizant that the real problem isn't the situation; the problem is *us*.

The sobering truth is that most of us make these decisions without realizing the significant impact they have on our lives. We don't realize that by having the neutral attitude of "I'm not sure," we are continually giving up on ourselves, turning back at just the critical moment, right before we would have succeeded. That hesitancy causes us to naturally gravitate away from making the commitment that's right in front of us and resets the cycle of us getting what we've always gotten.

> A life of average, or a life of mediocre, doesn't come from having a bad attitude. A life of *average* comes from having an *average* attitude.

Perhaps the most startling realization in my own life is that a life of average, or a life of mediocrity, doesn't come from having a bad attitude. A life of *average* comes from having an *average* attitude. It leaves me always just barely "a day late and a dollar short" because *average* comes as an unnoticeable by-product of always asking the question "Should I?" If you've ever felt frustrated that you're someone who just never seems to catch that big break, you know all too well what I mean.

Plunging Ahead

Committed, successful, disciplined people approach the decisional threshold almost imperceptibly different. Chances are that you follow this pattern in at least one area of your life.

To someone who is truly committed in an endeavor, there is no chance of turning back only because of the unacceptable consequences of doing so. At some point, either the stakes have become so high, or the person truly *decided* long ago that turning back just simply isn't an option.

As noted before, this person struggles with the expenditure of emotional energy in making a decision just like the average person would. But—and this is a big "but"—instead of saying, "I'm not sure yet," they say, "I'm in for

> Dormant forces, faculties, and talents become alive, and you discover yourself to be a greater person by far than you ever dreamed yourself to be.
> —*Patanjali*

good." That difference means that instead of being plagued by "Should I?" they have empowered themselves to ask, "How will I?"—"How will I make this relationship work?" "How will I get this done?"

One brilliant aspect of the human mind is that once we start asking the question "how," our creativity engages. As the second-century BC philosopher Patanjali said, "Your mind transcends limitations; your consciousness expands in every direction . . . Dormant forces, faculties, and talents become alive, and you discover yourself to be a greater person by far than you ever dreamed yourself to be."

In other words, when we intentionally ask "how" instead of settling for the default question of "should," our subconscious mind goes into overdrive, and we find ourselves answering those "how" questions—and achieving more than we ever thought possible.

The world of "how" opens up when you commit past that critical pivot point. It's why you hear so many speakers and teachers talk about how success is just beyond the point you feel like quitting. It's why Southwestern taught us that "the answer is always behind the next door." It's why almost everyone hits these decisional pivot points in their life that completely influence the

> If we aren't consciously choosing a good attitude, then we are unconsciously choosing a poor one.

trajectory of the rest of their life. Flipping the switch in that crucial moment is within your power—and can make all the difference, because if we aren't consciously choosing a good attitude, then we are unconsciously choosing a poor one. That is a choice in and of itself.

Creating Unacceptable Consequences

When I was a young boy, my brother Randy and I played football all the time. Well, we didn't really have a football, but we had a Garfield stuffed toy that someone had donated to us that was shaped like a football, and that was what we used. Other than Garfield's really big and hard plastic bug eyes that stung the crap out of your hands when someone threw it hard, it was the perfect football.

One place that we lived backed up to a house that had the scariest people you can imagine living in it. I don't know if you did this when you were kids, but we made up stories that these neighbors were ax murderers. They always wore dark clothes, only came out at night, and we were sure they were always peeking out the window.

We would say to each other, "I dare you to go ring their doorbell or knock on their door." Of course, we never actually did it because we were terrified. Until one day we were playing football, and when Randy threw the football to me, Garfield's bug eyes smacked off the palm of my hand and it went over the fence.

Even though we were young kids, the moment that Garfield went over the fence, our entire conversation shifted from "Should we go over there?" to "How are we going to get over there?" That moment is a classic example of a pivot point. It is the moment that you "throw the ball over the fence" and there is no choice but to figure out a way.

What ball do *you* need to throw over the fence? How can you increase your commitment to something you know needs to be done even though you're not yet sure if or how you'll be able to do it? How can you create an unacceptable consequence that will compel you to take action?

When Bob was standing in front of the urinal trying to decide what he was going to do, he created an unacceptable consequence. Losing $5 wasn't a big enough pain to Bob to leverage him to the point where he'd stick his hand into a public urinal. But losing $50 was!

As the $5 was lying in the urinal, Bob was at the pivot point. He was stuck in the emotional conundrum of what to do. It was a conundrum because there wasn't *clearly* a right decision to make. Losing $5 is a bummer, but so is sticking your hand in the toilet. In choosing between the $5 and sticking his hand in the toilet, Bob's internal question is "Should I?" "Should I get my money back?" "Should I stick my hand in there?" As in "Is it worth it?" or "Could I really do this?"

However, once Bob took out his $50 bill and threw it into the urinal, he *created* an unacceptable consequence and the decision became very clear. Suddenly his question changed from "*Should* I try to get my money back?" to "*How* am I going to get my money back?" It is that shift in mind-set that makes all the difference.

In fact, you may have already experienced this principle in your life in some fashion. Have you ever hired a personal trainer? Why do people hire personal trainers? Because if you don't feel like going to the gym, then you're not going to go, because it's not that big of a deal not to go. But once you are paying $150 per session whether you show up or not, you are going to be there!

> Changing from the question "Should I?" to "How will I?" is the mind-set shift that makes all the difference.

It's the same reason people hire personal coaches. Sure, they pay us for our skill and expertise. But they also pay us because it amplifies the unacceptable consequence of not making the changes they seek in their lives.

Now you might say, "But Rory, what about that expensive piece of exercise equipment I bought? That cost me good money and now I don't even use it." You're absolutely right. After a time, the consequence becomes less and less *unacceptable*. Plainly, it becomes more acceptable because enough time has passed that the sting of the pain is gone.

This points to another important characteristic of unacceptable consequences: They must be ongoing. The reason that hiring a trainer or a coach works better than buying new exercise equipment is because theoretically paying a trainer never stops, but paying for exercise equipment does. Consequences that are ongoing have more teeth.

Likewise, with every moment that passes by, the sting of the consequence has less and less impact on us. If Bob were to walk away from that $5 in the urinal, with each passing moment the likelihood of him returning to get it would be less and less. He would think about it less and less, its relevance to him would be less and less, and then eventually it would just slip away. That is exactly the same dynamic that happens in our relationships to our goals, our dreams, and the people we love; without commitment, they slip away.

Unfortunately, what's also true is that it's not just if Bob walks away that he becomes less likely to figure it out, but with every second that goes by that he thinks about it, he becomes less likely to commit to it. Because while he sits there thinking about it, he is in the mind-set of "Should I?" and if he is asking that question, then that means he is of the attitude "I'm not sure yet." And thus with each moment, he slips farther and farther away from crossing the pivot point.

If you are at a pivot point in your life and you truly want to make a change, then you must act now. You must increase the stakes, raise the price, and increase the amount of time and money you are investing into whatever it is that matters to you. Because if you don't shift from "I'm not sure yet" to "I am in for good," then you are already naturally slipping back into doing things the way you have always done them.

And realize that indecision often costs you more than the wrong decision does. Or as my friend and pastor at Cross Point Church in Nashville, Pete Wilson, says, "The cost of missing out is more than the cost of messing up."

Unconditional Commitment

Anyone who's made it to adulthood—or is well on their way there—knows that emotions, impulses, and circumstances are perpetually changing. Nothing stays the same for long. If our commitments are dependent on the alignment of such fickle criteria, then we're going to have a difficult life of up and down, to and fro; in short, we will live life as a should-head.

For example, in marriage we say, "I do until death do us part," but in all too many cases what we're really saying is, "I do until . . ."

- You get fat.
- You make less money.
- You cheat on me.

- The kids are grown.
- One of us meets someone else.

Or "I do as long as . . ."

- We have money.
- We have great sex.
- We're happy.
- It's convenient.

I wouldn't pretend to know which of these "outs" are okay and which aren't. My point is simply that most of us have these clauses or "conditions" in our commitments. They are unwritten and unspoken, but nevertheless they are almost always there. The evidence is in the excuses we make when we break our commitments. The excuses we give after the fact are the unverbalized "conditions" that have been there all along.

The good news is that your commitments can be independent of those ever-changing variables. Remember a commitment is just simply about asking yourself the question "How will I?" instead of "Should I?" The moment a spouse starts asking the question "Should I stay or go?" is the moment the marriage is really in trouble.

What conditions are *you* allowing to weaken commitments that should be ironclad?

UNWAVERING BELIEF

Case Study: Sue Schick, Healthcare,

Philadelphia, Pennsylvania

It's not always easy for a woman to rise to the very top of corporate America. What if I told you there was a woman who is among the top-level executives at one of America's largest companies, overseeing a division that serves approximately 1 million people through a team of 3,000 employees in ten offices across two states?

That's exactly what one of our coaching clients—Sue Schick, CEO of UnitedHealthcare of Pennsylvania and Delaware—has done. Oh, and she's done it in less than eight years with the company.

A Fortune 50 company, UnitedHealth Group is a diversified health and well-being company dedicated to helping people live healthier lives and making health care work better. Of its top thirty executives, six are women, including UnitedHealthcare's national CEO Gail Boudreaux, and Sue is one of the newest.

Sue attributes her professional and personal success to one core principle: commitment. However, she learned the value of commitment far away from any boardroom or meeting.

My son George was born with a serious birth defect—he was born without ears. As a new mom, I felt overwhelmed. And yet, my dad had instilled in me an unwavering belief that there is always a way. We were committed to finding a way for George to have normal hearing. Over the next seven years, it took four surgeons, two hospitals, and seven surgeries, but finally they were able to build him new ears and restore his hearing by the time he was eight years old.

So it was almost crushing when eight years later, his new ears failed, and George lost his hearing again. This time the best surgeons in the country told us definitively that there was no possible way that George's hearing would ever be saved. After countless doctor visits, thousands of dollars, and running on an emotionally empty gas tank, we were discouraged.

And then, again, I remembered my dad's advice: There is always a way when you are committed. Our family refused to give up hope and relentlessly held on to a conviction that we were going to find a way because it simply was not an option for George to live his life without hearing. We kept telling the doctors, "Thank you, we appreciate your time but we're going somewhere else until we find a cure." Nearly a decade later, we were able to track down the original specialist who was, yet again, able to work some magic.

I think after hearing the opinions of the "brightest doctors" in the world, most people would have accepted their prognosis, but to us, that was unacceptable. We were committed to finding a solution even if it took years to achieve the outcome we wanted— which it did.

The entire episode imprinted on me that it is the way I should live my life—at home and in business. Today George has fully restored hearing. He graduated from the University of Michigan, and has his first job.

It sometimes would be so easy to give in to the circumstances that we face in our lives, especially when emotions run high. But for our family, we know that with enough resilience, enough innovation, and enough focus, there is always a way.

You have to be so focused on finding a way that you don't even pay attention to the normal obstacles that slow most people down.

Conditional Commitment

I'm not suggesting that *every* commitment should be unconditional. There is nothing wrong with a conditional commitment as long as the parties involved have a reasonable understanding of what the boundaries are. Conditional commitments allow us to have flexibility in our lives, and to be involved in many different activities.

We can still be incredibly committed even if our commitments have some conditions to them. There is power in knowing our limitations, however. The foundation of a disciplined life is integrity and doing what we say we're going to do. If we state our conditions in advance, then we know they are legitimate and everyone can plan accordingly.

Crush It Where You're At

One of the most common questions I get asked, whether it's about a job or relationship or some other life decision, is "Rory, when do I know if I should leave to try something new?"

My response is almost always the same, and it's very simple: "Have you maximized your potential in the current situation?" If the answer is yes, and you are at the top of that profession, for example, and you feel like leaving, then go ahead. If the answer is no, then go to work until you do—and *then* evaluate the decision.

If you're not maximizing your potential where you are, then you can never know if you should leave because you haven't experienced all that it has to offer. Another way of thinking about it is that your decision will look much different after you've committed and played wholeheartedly, with full effort, than it does right now. Without ever doing that, it's not fair to yourself or the other people involved to leave your current situation.

It's interesting to note that successful people tend to be

successful everywhere they go, in whatever they do. For example, with enough time and training, a top realtor could probably become a top financial advisor, even if it isn't her most natural vocation. Michael Jordan is a great example of this. Basketball was his God-given gift and he might not have been able to master something else the way he mastered basketball, but the discipline and commitment he had makes him a pretty darn good baseball player—and golfer, too.

This explains why Vince Lombardi said, "Winning is a habit; unfortunately so is losing." Some people have the habit of victory and success, and although we'd like to believe that these people have a glamorizing mystical power, the truth is much more basic than that: They commit to whatever it is they want to do. If you ask me, that is the more impressive part—that they can commit and exercise self-discipline in just about anything they do.

So, you must crush it where you're at. You must dominate whatever it is that you are doing. You must do everything in your power to reach the top of whatever game it is you are playing. Because if you don't, then you are not a successful person looking for a new challenge to take on; you're a person with conditional commitment looking for a new set of circumstances, and most likely starting the same self-defeating pattern all over again.

Success isn't a matter of circumstance; it's a matter of choice. Finding new circumstances won't make you successful, but making new choices will.

The Commitment Continuum Applied: Choosing Your Attitude

Awhile back, my wife and I traveled to Jamaica. We landed at the airport only to face a torrential downpour. I must admit that it immediately caused me to have a negative attitude—or negatude, as my buddy Andy likes to call it for short. By the time we got into the cab, I was already in a pretty bad mood and frustrated that our relaxation time might be getting sabotaged by unruly weather patterns.

So I said to the cab driver, "What's with all the rain? Is it supposed to rain all week?" And this tall, dark Jamaican man looked back at me, smiled, and with a heavy accent said, "In Jamaica, man, we don't have rain; we only have . . . liquid sunshine, man."

Then as we were driving through town toward our hotel, I noticed that there were speed bumps everywhere. Again, I was growing frustrated and so I asked the driver, "What's with all the speed bumps? They're kind of annoying!" Again looking back in a jovial spirit he replied, "In Jamaica, man, we don't have speed bumps, we only have . . . sleeping police, man."

He went on to explain that apparently there had been a lot of children killed by people driving their cars recklessly down the city streets. In an effort to create a solution, the people in the area banded together to rally support for installing speed bumps to slow down dangerous drivers. Ever since, they have referred to them as the sleeping police.

In that moment, tired and wet, hot and disheveled, I realized for the first time what the true definition of attitude is. I've had the good fortune of being mentored by some of the greatest speakers in the world, all whom talk in some fashion about attitude, but it was a Jamaican cab driver, in a casual conversation, who finally got through to me.

Attitude is simply the way you *choose* to see things. What was rain to me was liquid sunshine to him. And what was a speed bump to me was a lifesaving device to him. It is important to notice how two people can look at the exact same thing and see it differently. And since how we see things affects how we feel and act, these choices, which might seem trivial, in fact have enormous power.

Another illustration of the difference our simple choices can make comes in a powerful book by Mac Anderson and Sam Parker called *212: The Extra Degree*. In the book, and a corresponding short video, the authors demonstrate the fact that at 211 degrees water is hot—but at 212 degrees it boils.

"With boiling water comes steam; and steam can power a locomotive. It's that 1 degree that makes all the difference,"

> Attitude is simply the way you *choose* to see things.

the authors say. They go on to illustrate the impact of 1 degree through several life examples.

I believe it is *that* 1 degree that is the minuscule, almost unnoticeable, nearly invisible, yet tantamount difference between choosing an attitude that says, "I'm not sure yet," and one that says, "I'm in for good." That is, one that asks, "Should I?" versus one that asks, "How will I?"

This 1-degree difference of commitment distinguishes which people you can count on and which ones will flake out on you.

It determines whom the world will say yes to and to whom the world will say no.

It is this difference that causes some to leave a lasting legacy while others are just a fleeting shadow of compromised potential.

It empowers us to live a life dictated by choices rather than one that is ruled by circumstances.

It enables us to develop momentum and resolve or to become subject to resistance and worry.

It dictates whether our life will be one of straightforward consistency or one of complicated indecision.

It foreshadows who will be married to their commitments and who will suffer divorce from their dreams.

It creates the marginal separation, which eventually turns into a gaping crevasse segregating the winners from the losers.

It is the "it factor" that will ultimately decide whether you are a success or a failure in life.

Commitment may sound hard, and it is, but it is necessary because no one ever said that self-discipline was supposed to be easy.

Or is it . . .

To see videos corresponding with this chapter, visit www.takethestairsbook.com/buyinprinciple.

3

FOCUS

THE MAGNIFICATION PRINCIPLE

f you were to lay a piece of paper down on the asphalt on a hot summer day, nothing would happen to it, but if you held a magnifying glass between the piece of paper and the sun, the paper would catch on fire.

Why? Because focus is literally power. Sunlight focused enough creates enough energy to set a piece of paper on fire. Water focused enough, or streamlined enough, can cut through steel. The Magnification Principle of Focus simply states one of life's most important truths, that *Focus Is Power*.

An essential step toward improving our self-discipline is improving our focus. When we have diluted focus, we get diluted results. Another way of looking at it is minimizing the amount of distraction that occurs in life.

Three Types of Procrastination

In the opening chapter, we looked at how procrastination costs employers more than $10,000 per year per employee. However, procrastination might be affecting you in more ways than you think.

> When we have diluted focus, we get diluted results.

There are three basic types of procrastination. The first is *classic procrastination*. This is consciously delaying what we know we should be doing. You may or may not be willing to admit that you struggle with this problem, but most of us do in at least one area of our life.

For example, you might be very efficient at work, but when it comes to paying your bills, you almost always let them pile up until they're out of control. Or perhaps your finances are in order, but you always seem to find ways of putting off cleaning up around the house. Or maybe you have all of those things going well for you but you can't get yourself to the gym even though you know you need to go.

There is, however, a more dangerous type of procrastination that's increasingly prevalent in the workplace today. It's dangerous because it is *unconscious*—subtle and invisible, yet all too real in terms of the damage it wreaks. It's a pattern of behavior I first diagnosed in myself, and I call it *creative avoidance*.

Creative avoidance is unconsciously filling the day with menial work to where we end up getting busy just being busy! When I discovered this problem for myself, I realized that all day long I would be answering emails, pushing paper, chitchatting with coworkers, spacing out, running personal errands, and so on. At the end of the day I had "worked" all day long, but didn't have much to show for it.

I was engaged in activities all day, but I wasn't making progress. I was being efficient, but I wasn't being effective. I was doing things right, but I wasn't doing the right things. As the old anonymous quote goes, "In the absence of disciplined focus, we become strangely loyal to performing daily acts of trivia."

> In the absence of disciplined focus, we become strangely loyal to performing daily acts of trivia.

The real danger to creative avoidance is that there is no end to it. It can go on and on and forever. As the Law of Douglas McArthur states, "The amount of busy work will always expand to fulfill the amount of free time available."

I was consumed with creative avoidance. I was putting off the things I knew were most important and defaulting to easier activities that required less mental energy and were, of course, less productive. It was a form of taking the escalator.

Are you able to relate with this concept of creative avoidance? Are there ever times when you become obsessed with minutiae while ignoring what's truly important? Most of us do, as it is the way of the "escalator world." We tell ourselves we're busy, but in fact, we're spending hours surfing online, watching reruns, or creating "make work" for ourselves, while the real work goes ignored.

If there isn't a defined objective or outcome for the activities you're engaged in, stop doing them! If you feel that your life is being pulled toward the mindless minutiae of everyday life, wake up! How sad it is that so many of our goals and dreams eventually give way to the meandering and the mundane. The choice is ours.

The third type of procrastination is another one that often goes unnoticed—and it tends to affect the very people who aim to achieve. It's called "priority dilution."

Priority dilution is most commonly found in high-performing people—the ones who are the most busy, competent, and overwhelmed. They know what their goals are—but they nonetheless allow their attention to shift to less important tasks. They have so many emails, meetings, objectives, family matters, and other responsibilities on their plate that they can start to lose control of their effectiveness.

How often do you get to every email in your in-box? Umm, never?

For example, when it comes to catching up on work, this type of busy, overwhelmed person will almost always try to tame their email in-box by starting at the top and working their way down. Needless to say, this is an unreliable approach, and far from a foolproof system. (How often do you get to every email in your in-box? Umm, never?)

While someone with "creative avoidance" takes things that aren't important and makes them urgent, a person struggling with priority dilution takes things that are urgent and inappropriately makes them important. As my friend the author David Allen describes, "Rather than doing what we know needs to be done, we're constantly falling victim to whatever is latest and loudest."

Our experience coaching hundreds of clients is that for today's intellectual workforce, discipline is about focusing on what's most important, learning to let go of minutiae, and being okay with delaying the less important tasks to an appropriate time (more on that when we discuss the Harvest Principle).

As it turns out, the most important skill for the next generation of knowledge worker is not learning what *to do* but rather determining what *not to do*. And instead focusing on key objectives. Peace of mind comes from falling in love with the fact that there is simply and certainly always going to be more to do than we have time for. It's only as we embrace the incredible volume of noise in our work and our

> The most important skill for the next generation of knowledge worker is not learning what *to do* but rather determining what *not to do*.

lives that we can silence it—or at least reduce it to a dull roar. *Ignore the noise. Conquer the critical. Manage the minutiae.*

To achieve the focus we so vitally need, we need to manage three essential aspects of ourselves: our thoughts, our words, and our behavior. I address all three in this book, but we start by learning to focus our thinking because mastery of our mind precedes the movement of our bodies. And permanent changes in our actions have to be reinforced by permanent changes in our thinking.

Focusing Our Thoughts

The hit book and movie *The Secret* did a dazzling job of reeducating the world about an essential principle of success: *We become what we think about.* What we focus on we tend to bring about.

The frightening truth is that when we're not thinking about our thinking, our thinking starts to think on its own.

As many of us now know, it's called the Law of Attraction, and it's not a magical, cosmic, mystical force at work. Rather, it's a demonstration of the power of our subconscious mind—a power that yields tremendous results, if we focus and monitor our thoughts using a Take the Stairs approach.

In today's escalator world, most of us don't have to think much. We have cell phones that remember important phone numbers, we turn to the Internet whenever we have a question, and we rely on fast food and other modern conveniences to satisfy our basic needs. The danger, though, is that we *are always thinking*. We just haven't been thinking about it. The frightening truth is that when we're not thinking about our thinking, our thinking starts to think on its own.

Psychologists say that the human mind thinks seven times faster than we can talk and yet so many of us allow our most powerful asset to wander aimlessly free in whatever direction is most convenient at the moment.

I can't speak for your mind, but I can say with absolute certainty that in the absence of constant monitoring, my mind naturally gravitates toward the negative. In fact, my unmonitored thoughts are often so negative that I've come to believe that I'm not the only person influencing my thoughts but rather that there is another person influencing them, too.

Enter my little voice, Mr. M.

From the time you were born, you have not been alone. You have had with you your entire life a little companion. Dan Moore, President of Southwestern, says that this little companion, who sits on your shoulder, is so small that he's invisible, but somehow his mouth is huge. This companion is commonly known as "your little voice." If you just sit still in the quiet for a moment, you will hear him.

"What little voice? I don't have a little voice. This guy's a loon. Take the stairs? I'm not going to take the stairs. We have escalators for a reason."

You see, that's your little voice. Some people get confused that it's "you" but that's not "you" because if that is "you," then who the heck is he talking to?

No, that's not you, that's your little voice. Let's call him Mr. M. And for some reason Mr. M was programmed from birth with one objective: to ruin your positive momentum. Mr. M whines, complains, sees the negative, and always points out every reason and everything about why things aren't going to work out the way you want them to. His only focus is to make sure that you live a life of average, a life of comfortable, a life of mediocrity. That's why we at Southwestern like to call him "Mr. Mediocrity."

There are certain times in your life when Mr. Mediocrity gets going like crazy. Anytime things are physically uncomfortable, when you think creatively about new endeavors, and oftentimes when you're around your in-laws. As humorous as the idea of Mr. Mediocrity is, don't misunderstand me; he is alive and well and he was born very negative. One of the most difficult tasks in building up your integrity and maintaining your commitment to Take the Stairs is to learn to get control over Mr. Mediocrity.

Almost all of the world's ultrasuccessful people agree that the best way to get control of Mr. Mediocrity is to learn to master your positive self-talk. Although he has a big mouth, it's nearly impossible for him to talk over you. You see, it's virtually impossible for you to be saying something positive and thinking something negative. Try it. If you just start saying out loud, "I can, I will, I'm going to; I can, I will, I'm going to," over and over, it's almost impossible for Mr. Mediocrity to chime in with his negative opinions.

If you're going to Take the Stairs and you're going to be successful, you have to learn to discipline yourself to use positive affirmations. Train your mind so that every time you hear Mr. Mediocrity going off about something, your personal alarm will sound and you will immediately exterminate his fire by spraying it with a blast of positive self-talk. This will feel stupid at first. Actually, it might always feel a little silly. I will tell you right now that most people do not *want* to use positive affirmations. But remember: Successful people do what others don't feel like doing—and that is why they get extra*ordinary* results.

How much of your life has been dictated by your Mr. Mediocrity? How many times have you indulged in something just because Mr. Mediocrity wouldn't shut up? How many times have you hurt someone, offended someone, or said something you didn't really mean but it came out because Mr. Mediocrity was flapping his yap over and over in your ear? If you're like the rest of us, it probably happens quite often and we've

allowed Mr. Mediocrity to dictate how we're feeling and then we respond and make decisions based on *feelings*.

One paramount advantage of using positive self-talk is that it has the ability to change how you're feeling. As the inspiring author Og Mandino wrote, "If you are depressed, start singing." If you feel underconfident, speak powerfully. If you are unsure, then use your words to immediately create a possibility for you to live into. It is this skill that will enable you to literally control your emotions. Positive affirmations give you the power to cause physiological change in the way you are feeling at any given moment.

Learn to discipline the use of your words and to use positive affirmations when Mr. Mediocrity gets going. The best book on this topic is *What to Say When You Talk to Yourself* by Shad Helmstetter. Get it. Read it. Live it. It will help you form the habits that will enable you to Take the Stairs. It will walk you through step-by-step how to get control over Mr. Mediocrity and how to regain control of your thinking.

CRYSTAL CLEAR THINKING

Case Study: Synara Brown, Mom (who happens to be in direct sales), Milwaukee, Wisconsin

Obviously, finding the right things to eat to stay healthy is a challenge for all of us. One company has turned it into an explosive growth party-plan business. Wildtree makes all-natural food completely free of any additives, preservatives, MSGs, dyes, etc. They have everything from dips and dressings to pizza and pancakes—and it's all delicious. Of the 3,500 active reps who have made a part-time business opportunity out of it, one mom is personally responsible for having built an organization of more than 2,100 of them.

Synara Brown says she joined Wildtree because she wanted to put her family first, and while doing that, she has also managed to create an income for herself that rivals most corporate executives. How does she run such a huge organization and still catch every one of her kids' field trips? She humbly says:

The only thing I might do differently than everyone else is I know exactly what I want and I'm focused on why I'm doing it. I have such a clearly defined reason for success that I'm excited to do it!

When people can't get themselves to do the things they don't want to do, it's only because they don't have a strong enough why. If they can't find the motivation to work or make phone calls, it's because they haven't taken the time to clearly define their overall purpose. They don't have a strong enough vision to leverage against the sacrifices that are required to get there.

Instead, most people have distracted thinking and rarely put in an honest day's work. Most people spend ten to fifteen hours a week watching TV. I don't watch TV. I can get most of my work done in a couple hours a day if I'm doing the right things, and then I spend the rest of my time with my family.

Given the dramatic size of her organization, I asked Synara how she keeps up with all of them. She said:

I don't. I spend time with my best leaders, and they do a better job than I could of coaching their most disciplined people. I can tell within two weeks if someone has what it takes to be successful, because it shows up right away in their follow-through, their attitude, and their work ethic. All of which are by-products of someone who is simply in control of their thoughts and has a clear and compelling vision.

Visioneering

Focusing our thoughts is the entry point for all creation in our entire life. Before we create anything in our physical world, it first must be conceived in our mental world. Some people call it purpose, some call it vision, and some call it possibility. The term I prefer is "visioneering." I got the term from author Andy Stanley and I love it because it appropriately accounts for the two most critical aspects of creating a new idea—"vision" and "engineering."

Regardless of whether you call it a goal, a purpose, or a vision, the bottom line is that you need to have one. Developing a vision isn't an academic exercise, it's not an element of a business plan, and it's also not a metaphysical meeting with the universe. A vision is an inspiring mental picture that propels you to take action. Your vision is important because the amount of your endurance, and the intensity of your focus, is directly proportionate to the clarity of your vision.

> The amount of your endurance, and the intensity of your focus, is directly proportionate to the clarity of your vision.

The more clearly you see your vision, the more you can focus on it, and the more you focus on it, the more it draws you to action. A great vision is like a powerful magnet pulling you into a future of becoming a better you.

The power that a clear picture of your desired future has over your life is indescribable. The moment you capture a detailed vision in your brain, your physical body starts to respond immediately. It's imperative that you not underestimate the power of this mental picture and its connection to the physical world you will create for yourself.

"Nocturnal Emissions"

The person who broke through my natural skepticism about the power and importance of these vivid mental declarations was my Frederick High School basketball coach, Terry Witty. Coach Witty was known for being a traditional disciplinarian. While he didn't always have the most finesse in his communication (He used to yell at me, "Vaden!! You are the damn dumbest smart kid I've ever met!"), he was another incredibly important role model who helped shape the way I think today.

When Coach first told me about this mental picture stuff, I thought it was total nonsense; until he was able to relate the concept to our entire team in terms we understood: He used the example of nocturnal emissions.

Coach addressed our team and said, "Many of you young men have already realized the power of mental visualizations because you've had, as many teenage boys do, what I like to call nocturnal emissions." Let me just say that as a group of young men, we *got* it.

Another, more G-rated example is a nightmare. Have you ever woken up in the middle of the night with a racing heart and a cold sweat? These two simple examples illustrate how powerful our thoughts can be, bringing about real, physiological change. It's up to us to harness this power to bring about the most important changes we want in our lives.

My Life, Visioneered

On October 27, 2005, I sat down and wrote out a detailed description of what I wanted my life to look like. I had just learned about a contest called the World Championship of Public Speaking, hosted by Toastmasters International. It's a contest where 30,000 people from more than 113 countries compete over nine months to make it to the finals as one of the ten best speakers in the world.

In the middle of the night I woke up with a sharp feeling that I was supposed to pursue the contest. I'd had visions like this as a child—of getting my black belt, becoming valedictorian, and getting a full scholarship to college—but this was the clearest picture I'd ever had in my life.

The vision seemed so overwhelmingly impossible that it brought me to the point of tears because the youngest person ever to win the contest had been twenty-nine years old. I was twenty-three.

Much of what was about to be a long journey had been spurred by a professional speaker I had gotten to know, a man named Eric Chester. I'd long dreamed about being a professional speaker, but it wasn't until that meeting with Eric that I saw what the path looked like. He said that the difference between a good speaker and a great speaker is 1,000 presentations. He told me to join Toastmasters and to speak as much as I could, anywhere someone would let me. My decision to join Toastmasters ended up changing the course of my life forever.

As I started writing about winning the contest, I described the scene of what it would look like. I described how I would feel. I also started writing about what my lifestyle would be like.

I wrote this long list about speaking in front of thousands of people with a message of self-discipline. I wrote about waking up on the top story of a downtown loft, and going to work as an executive of a large speaking and training company. Included in my write-up were the names of twelve people that I looked up to that I said I wanted to be close friends with. There was also a list of seven accomplishments, including writing a bestselling book.

At the end was a statement that said, "Success is never owned, it is rented, and the rent is due every day—the only question now is am I willing to pay a price that is greater than everyone else?"

As I wrote those words, I was living in a crappy apartment on the second floor of an old building. I was finishing up graduate school at the University of Denver, working for an Internet security company, had briefly met one of the people in my vision, and had never given a professional speech in my life.

Over the next eighteen months I spoke 304 times for free at

churches, comedy clubs, Toastmasters meetings, high schools, and anywhere else that would give me time. I spent hundreds of hours and thousands of dollars getting coaching and reading books on success and the speaking profession.

Toastmasters across the country invited me to their clubs and gave me free evaluations and coaching; Toastmasters lifted me up. Speakers like Eric, David Avrin, Darren LaCroix, and Mark Sanborn from the National Speakers Association took me under their wing and showed me the ropes; they believed in me.

On August 15, 2007, I became the youngest person in history to place second at the Toastmasters International World Championship of Public Speaking. On April 27, 2007, I bought a condo on the twenty-ninth floor of a building in downtown Nashville with one of my business partners. At the time this book was written, we celebrated the five-year anniversary of our global training and coaching company, Southwestern Consulting, which is a multimillion-dollar business operating in three countries. Today eight of the twelve people on the original list are close friends of mine. Five of the seven accomplishments on my list have been achieved, and you're holding the book in your hand, which—depending on how sales are going—hopefully becomes number six.

It came to pass faster than I could have imagined, and much of it had to do with the clarity and specificity with which I saw the vision and my ability to focus on it. This is simply a personal testimony to the power of focus—a power that is immediately available to you by simply focusing on and being intentional about controlling your own thoughts. One thing that is certain is we definitely don't pay *attention* to things we don't first give our *intention* to.

> We don't pay *attention* to things we don't first give our *intention* to.

How clear is your vision? What do you want? If you could live any type of lifestyle, what would it look like? Isn't it worth the time to write it out?

Make Your Visions VAST

A practical technique that I adapted from friend and World Champion speaker, Craig Valentine, is to make your declarations, intentions, and possibilities VAST. That is, describe and write out your vision using words that appeal to the senses: Visual, Auditory, Smell, and Touch. Adding this simple technique to the way you create your visions will make them more visceral, activating your senses and increasing their power.

Put effort and care into writing your visions. Since it's your entire future on the line, have the discipline to spend some energy doing it right and pretend as if you are an author describing the most vivid possible scenery for your reader. Except that the scene you're describing is your life's mission and the reader is you. Making a vision VAST will help it come alive for you.

Vision Boards

Nearsightedness is one of the leading causes of failure in our escalator world. We spend so much of our time mindlessly wandering through the infinite minutiae in our life that we easily lose sight of the overall direction we should be moving. One ageless technique of the most successful people in the world is to create a vision board.

Vision boards have also become popular in recent years. They are very simple. You collect pictures or images from the Internet, in magazines, or anywhere else, and you create a collage of the things you hope to manifest in your life. This technique is powerful because it enables you to quickly remind yourself of the things that you want, and to *experience* them as emotional triggers.

This was yet another gimmicky-sounding idea that I never wanted to do because it seemed so cheesy, but I gave it a try when I learned that so many rich and successful people have done so. After all, a Take the Stairs mind-set involves doing things most people don't want to. As it turns out, vision boards have become one of the most influential components of my life.

In fact, in our new house we custom-built a vision board box right into the wall!

It's truly amazing how many of the items on my boards and those of our coaching clients have manifested almost exactly as they were laid out. Crafting a vision board is the first and most important exercise we do when someone enters into our coaching program. We update the pictures every couple of months to keep them fresh and inspiring. Try it for yourself. You won't be sorry.

First In, Last Out

Finally, one of the most important ways to focus your thoughts is to make your very first and last thoughts of the day ones that inspire and motivate you. Typically, I'll read a few pages of a good book at night, and as soon as my eyes get tired, I'll put my book down and allow my mind to wander into a vivid visualization of the things that I want most in my life.

It's equally important that you are deliberate with the first few thoughts you allow to enter your mind right when you wake up in the morning. Those first few thoughts have a lot to do with dictating your attitude throughout that day. Per the suggestion again of Darren Hardy, publisher and editorial director of *Success* magazine, I hit snooze one time each morning but stay awake in bed for ten minutes vividly picturing all of the things I'm thankful for in my life. That exercise combined with a few minutes of reading the Bible or some other reading that gives you spiritual rejuvenation right when you wake up can be enough to powerfully change the course of your day—and your life. It starts with thinking about your thinking and focusing on your focus.

Visioneering in Action

What do you see for your future? What matters most to you? What would you want your perfect life to look like? What is it that you want to have? What things do you want to do?

Focus on them. Think about them. Affirm in your mind, on paper, and out loud your ability to achieve them. By consciously shaping your thoughts, you'll be consciously shaping your attitude. Once you have a strong attitude, then sound actions are guaranteed. With sound actions taking place, success and real results are inevitable.

It's a shame that we spend years of our life doing activities we think we're supposed to do, and we spend only minutes figuring out what we really want.

It's a shame that we spend years of our life doing activities we think we're supposed to do, and we spend only minutes figuring out what we really want. Start writing now.

If you haven't already, take "The Focused 40" quiz at www.takethestairsbook.com/focused40.

4

INTEGRITY

THE CREATION PRINCIPLE

n the beginning was the Word, and the Word was with God, and the Word was God. He was with God in the beginning. Through him all things were made; without him nothing was made that has been made. In him was life, and that life was the light of men." Regardless of your religious beliefs, there's no denying the power and prominence the books of Genesis and John give to the spoken word. Quite literally, God *spoke* the world into existence.

You and I have the power to author change in our lives by first carefully choosing our words and then living into them.

One of the major causes of pain in today's escalator world is that most people don't realize the *impact* of their words on themselves and others. Words have power—the power to add meaning, and the power to diminish meaning. The power to give life, and the power to take it away.

The Creation Principle of Integrity states that all of creation follows a simple and powerful pattern: *You think it, you speak it, you act it, it happens.*

From the chair that you are sitting in, to the tallest building on the planet, to the company that you work for, to all of the media you digest, this simple pattern is replicated over and over. Words are the engine that sets actions in motion. As with our thoughts, they carry

> You think it, you speak it, you act it, it happens.

tremendous power if they are chosen with care and intention. Having a strong word is the absolute foundation of a disciplined life. With concrete integrity, you can create *anything* you want for your life.

"Do I Have a Dad?"

When I was seven years old, I was driving with my mom on South Boulder Road heading into Boulder, Colorado. It's one of the most amazing scenes on the planet because, when you drive from Louisville into Boulder, there is this point where you come over a hill and the entire Rocky Mountains open up to you.

Across this beautiful landscape you can see the snowcapped mountains and let crisp mountain air rejuvenate your lungs as you rush down this enormous hill. I very specifically remember this time in my life not because of the scenery but because I remember turning to my mom and asking her these questions.

"Mom, do I have a dad? Where is my dad? Other kids at school all have a dad. Where is my dad?"

My mom answered, "I've not had much luck with men, honey. I've tried a couple times and it never seems to work out well for us."

To which I responded, "Yeah, but I want a dad."

She replied, "Well then, honey, if you want a dad, then you're going to have to go find your own dad. Go find us a good one."

I remember thinking . . . "What kind of crap is that?! Find my own dad?" But I also remember taking it on as a personal challenge and declaring, "Okay, deal. I will find a dad for us."

On that drive we were heading to my very first day at a new Shaolin Kung Fu center. I had been doing Tae Kwon Do before that but was looking for a new challenge. What was unique about this Kung Fu center was that it was all adults. The youngest person there next to me was twenty-eight years old.

On my very first day, I got paired up with a man named Kevin who had also just joined the school. He had long hair and these big tattoos on his arms, and he wore this tattered leather jacket and drove a motorcycle. Let me just say that, to a seven-year-old, he was about the scariest person I had ever met!

Because we were both new to the class, we became sparring partners. As time went by, we started advancing through the belt levels together and became quite good friends. The higher the levels we reached, the later the classes were at night, and eventually he started bringing me home after class since Mom had to get up early to go to work.

Kevin started bringing me home at night and then he started hanging out with me on the weekends. Before I knew it, he and my mom and I were all hanging out together. And I'll never forget the first time they went to a movie—without me. I was pretty mad!

Eventually, I realized what was happening. When I was ten, Kevin and I tested for our black belts together; he and my mom got married shortly after. He adopted me, I changed my last name to his, and I have called him Dad ever since.

Had my mom and I never had that conversation, would they have ever met and fallen in love? There is no way to know for sure. But I do know that any creation in life follows a similar pattern. You think it, you speak it, you act, it happens. Our words, then, are incredibly important in shaping our lives. Choosing them with integrity is the fuel that will power us to Take the Stairs for life.

What would you create in your life if you knew you could start the process by simply speaking it into existence?

Positive Ways to Strengthen Your Word

There are a number of simple ways we can strengthen our words, adding to our integrity and maximizing their potential for positive change in our lives and the lives of others.

Inventing Possibility. After taking a powerful course called "Landmark Education," I learned that by making a statement of our intention to complete something, we are, in a sense, setting the stage to have it happen. In order for a change to take place, you must first *invent* the possibility of it actually happening by using your words. What changes do you want to bring about in your life? Start small, and as you gain confidence, you can make bigger and bigger verbal commitments. The common saying "Be careful what you wish for" applies here, though, because what you say is very likely to take shape. Choose your statements with care.

Expressing Gratitude. There is perhaps no better way to keep the tenacious Mr. Mediocrity, that little voice described in the previous chapter, at bay than expressing gratitude for the good fortune in your life. At any given moment we are either choosing to focus on what we're grateful for or we're worrying about the things we've not been given. Putting words to your gratitude erases frustration, and can jump-start your motivation to keep a Take the Stairs mind-set, even when the escalator world is calling to you.

Compliments. It is an interesting peculiarity of human nature that we have a deep fundamental desire to be *right*. Compliments are powerful because, when we genuinely acknowledge someone for an admirable trait or job well done, we satisfy their intrinsic appetite to be *right*. In this way, verbal appreciation is a form of currency. It is an unlimited resource that can be exchanged freely to create very strong bonds between two people.

> At any given moment we are either choosing to focus on what we're grateful for or we're worrying about the things we've not been given.

In a world of scarce appreciation, the unexpected dynamic that compliments create is one of endeared loyalty and positive change. By *speaking* to someone in an uplifting way, we directly *cause* sustainable modification in their behavior. As it was well stated by Christine Roland, one of our management coaching clients, "That which is recognized is repeated."

Yet all too often we underestimate the powerful impact of our words on other people's lives. But as observed by Christine, a tremendously successful manager in the logistics business, "When you speak to people not just for who they are but for who they can become, you create a positive way of *being* for them to live into in the future." By this rule, we think it, we speak it, *they* act, it happens.

Seeing People for Who They Can Become

During my time recruiting students to sell at Southwestern, one student who made a particularly strong impression on me was a young woman named Lara. From the first time we talked, she seemed to have an incredible potential for growth locked inside her, which for some reason had not yet come out. When she heard about the details of our summer program, she immediately knew that it was what she needed to do. Not for the money, but for her confidence. Everyone in the room could see the spark and feel the energy and the passion that had been ignited inside her.

I'll never forget the next day when Lara cried as she described to me how her family had told her no. She was crying because her friends told her "it wasn't a good idea." Most of all, she was crying because she didn't have enough confidence to know beyond a shadow of a doubt that she could participate in the program and be successful.

At some point during that conversation, one of our other young managers came by and said, "Lara! You can do this. You know you can work hard, and if you do that, then you'll win. You are the kind of person who has what it takes to make this happen."

Eight months later we were with Lara in Mexico on the free trip that she had won from having a successful first summer. Lara made some money, learned some valuable life skills, and met some new friends, but most of all she developed within herself a legitimate confidence from being able to do things that others weren't willing to do. Sparked by a validating compliment at just the right moment, Lara had liberated her potential.

Your conviction can easily become someone else's conviction when you have strong integrity. And paying someone the compliment of their life not only makes you both feel terrific, but also allows you to help contribute to a more powerful future.

Holding People Accountable. Many people would like to be held accountable to what is best for them, yet it can be hard to do that when nobody wants to be criticized—or to offer criticism to others. The most effective way to encourage positive change in this way is to remove our own judgments and feelings and simply commit to reminding the person of who they said they wanted to be. The danger is that we sometimes come across as though we've got something figured out that they don't, that they have made some kind of mistake, or that we are *right* and they are *wrong*.

In our experience working with clients one-on-one, we see consistently that what they want is a partner, not a persecutor. An effective accountability partner is someone who attacks the problem that is being dealt with, while supporting the person who is trying to make the change. We do this by saying things like:

- "I believe in you too much to watch you [insert activity]."
- "I know you well enough to know that you don't really want to [insert activity], but what you really want is [insert goal]."
- "[Insert name], you are an important person in my life and it wouldn't be right if I didn't tell you how disappointed it makes me when you [insert activity]."
- "Hopefully by now you realize that I want the absolute best for you. Because of that, I think it's only fair that I let you know that [insert activity] isn't acceptable to me because it doesn't help you get to where I know you want to be."
- "I am convinced that you have everything it takes to do well at [insert goal], and so I'd be letting you down if I didn't share with you how it makes me feel when you [insert activity]."

Also, keep in mind that there are three ways to get people to take action. The first is to ask them to do it. The second is to force them to do it. And the third is to help them recognize for themselves why it's in their best interest to take a certain course of action. If you can master the delicate balance of holding people accountable without holding them hostage, you will have dramatically increased your ability to facilitate change.

Walking the Walk. In the movie *Liar Liar*, Jim Carrey's character finds out that not only does he have to tell the truth, but he also can't ask questions when he knows the answer is going to be a lie. That is similar to the relationship of your word to what you ask of others. Being able to do what you say you're going to do isn't enough; you have to also not be willing to ask people to do things that you wouldn't do. Mastering this principle is critical to developing integrity as the foundation of a disciplined life.

> Hold people accountable without holding them hostage.

Negative Ways to Weaken Your Word

One of the greatest problems in the escalator world is a lack of integrity in the way most of us use our words. It comes from music, movies, people in the media, the Internet, and more. Having a Take the Stairs mind-set means recognizing and avoiding these common pitfalls.

Breaking Our Promises. When you break a promise, you let someone else down, and you also damage your own credibility. Every time you fail to come through on something you said you'd do, you weaken the power of your words to produce the results you want in the future. Any incongruence between our words and our actions directly impacts our ability to *create* as we move forward. Have you noticed more of this in these escalator times? It takes strength to Take the Stairs—but the effort is rewarded many times over.

Uncontrolled Language. One of the most common ways that people lack discipline with their words is by not thinking about their impact on others. What kind of language you use is up to you, but the discipline part comes in by crafting our words with care rather than simply disregarding how what we say might be affecting the people we're saying it to. Saying whatever we feel and think without first filtering it through the lens of how it might impact the people around us is not transparency; it's indulgence. I learned this lesson the hard way.

When I was a teenager, swearing seemed like cool adult behavior. I thought it was a way to assert power and freedom. As I was a fairly strong-willed and independent young lad, I formed the obscene-language habit early on; I thought it made me seem more mature. All that changed one day when I was fifteen years old. We were in the living room of my parents' house when my mom said, "You know, honey, it really hurts my feelings when you curse in front of me."

Wow. Painful. How embarrassing to feel like I was disappointing my mom because of my inability to exercise restraint over simple words. I decided right then and there that I would do my best never to curse in front of her ever again. A while later I decided that if it hurt her, it probably hurt others as well, so I stopped altogether. Lesson learned. Are you considerate of how your words are affecting the people around you?

Tearing Others Down. Dale Carnegie wrote decades ago, "Never say anything bad about anyone. Ever." This is one of the most powerful pieces of advice I've ever come across. Again, I don't make the case for moral purposes. You decide what is moral. I make the argument because of the negative impact it has on the foundation of your new life—your word. Another tremendous lesson I've learned in this regard is something that's often said in the speaking profession: "The microphone is always on." It's a reminder always to speak with care, and it's good advice given the advancement of technology and how easy it is for people to capture our words and have them etched permanently in Internet history.

Creating Back Doors. Undisciplined people are often afraid to make commitments. They are afraid to say "I will" or "I do" to most things. Because they don't have confidence that they will be able to follow through on their word, they create "back doors" or verbal and mental escape hatches so that they can abandon their commitments and still save face when they become inconvenient.

In Chapter 2, we discussed one of them, which is "as long as." Or perhaps you've heard people say things like, "I should be able to." Another common one is "I'll try to . . ."

Back doors are another form of taking the easy way out. It's taking the escalator. In the words of the great philosopher Yoda, "Do, or do not. But do not try."

A Take the Stairs mind-set means saying either "I will do _____ period," or "No, I'm sorry; I can't commit to that." Those two statements are much harder to make—and they are much more powerful. When it comes to making commitments to other people, sometimes one of the hardest things to learn to say is no when we mean no.

Previous Negation. In the same family as a "back door" is a previous negation. If "back doors" are most commonly characterized by saying "as long as," then a previous negation is identified most often by the word "but." Whenever you say the word "but," you are negating whatever you said before it.

One of the most damaging times to use the word "but" is when giving feedback or compliments. I often hear people say things like, "You were great, *but* if you could do _____ and _____, it would be better." The word "but" is a subconscious (and sometimes conscious) trigger to the listener that basically everything that came before that word was meaningless.

When we negate in this way, we might think we're softening our criticism, but in fact, we're weakening our compliment—and more important, we are weakening our word in general. Say what you mean, as directly as possible.

Gossip. One of the hardest forms of discipline to master, for myself and many others, is to avoid the indulgence of gossip. Gossip is all too easy to participate in. It's all around us, it's contagious, and it can seem harmless—but it's not. Gossip can destroy companies, destroy relationships, and even destroy families. It is one of the most destructive forces in the escalator world. Keep in mind that the consequences of gossip are not limited to just the instigator or the subject, but that it usually ends up negatively affecting those who are passing it along or even those trying to help by getting in the middle of it. When you discover that two people are in conflict, take charge of the situation by making them talk directly to one another. It's just one more way we can learn to get control of our word. We must get control of our word and our integrity before we can get control of our life.

Using Too Many Words. Mark Twain said, "Brevity is the essence of wisdom." John Maxwell calls it, "The Law of E. F. Hutton—when the real leader speaks, people listen." David Brooks says, "Tell people everything they need to know, and not a word more." I say that if someone has to talk a lot, they probably don't know what they really want to say. The most powerful people in the world listen first, process the information, and then respond.

> We must get control of our word and our integrity before we can get control of our life.

Less is almost always more. As James Humes once wrote, there are 66 words in the Lord's Prayer—most people know it. There are 179 words in the Ten Commandments—many people can recite them. There are 282 words in the Gettysburg

Address—a lot of Americans talk about it. And then there are 26,911 words . . . in the U.S. government's regulation on the sale of cabbage—and nobody cares.

Intellectual Dishonesty. This is perhaps the sneakiest and fastest-growing form of weakening word. Intellectual dishonesty isn't telling a lie. It isn't even saying something and not following through on it. Intellectual dishonesty is simply allowing someone to believe something that you know is not true.

Intellectual dishonesty is tricky to spot because it's not something that you say; it's what you don't say.

Personally, I've seen that intellectual dishonesty strikes two groups of people hardest: corporate executives and salespeople. We need look no further than the accounting scandals of the early twenty-first century to find prime examples of intellectual dishonesty. Executives allowed thousands of people to *think* that they were playing by the rules of accounting and that the monies they were in charge of were being handled with fiduciary responsibility. In most cases they didn't lie about where the money was going (although in some cases they did); rather, they simply allowed people to assume that everything was great when, in fact, it was not.

> Intellectual dishonesty is simply allowing someone to believe something that you know is not true.

Salespeople are faced with the escalator temptation of

intellectual dishonesty on a daily basis. Every time a prospect asks about a feature of your product that is available but limited (compared to, say, a competitor's), it's much easier for the salesperson to say, "Yeah, this does that, too," rather than explaining the actual limited functionality.

Recruiters are often faced with this challenge regularly as well. Imagine if a recruiter is hiring someone for a job, and in an interview the candidate says, "In my last job I had a 401(k) and my employer matched it. Do you have a 401(k)?" And let's say that the recruiter's company does offer a 401(k) but does not offer matching. Then it would be very easy for the recruiter to say, "Yeah, of course we have a 401(k)." The Take the Stairs approach requires responding with honesty and clarity, rather than allowing a more convenient half-truth to prevail.

I'm not saying it's easy, or even that I am always able to do this. I'm just saying these are the standards that the most successful people in the world seem to hold themselves up to—which we should all work to achieve.

PRIVATE VICTORIES

Case Study: Sean Wolfington, Automotive & Entertainment, Miami, Florida

What does selling cars have to do with producing blockbuster movies? Nothing, and that is exactly the point. Because if you are a creative genius like Sean Wolfington, you've reached a level of significance in both of those industries and built a $500 million empire in the process by implementing one consistent strategy: rock-solid integrity. "If there is one thing I do different than most people, it's that I see how things should be, and then I just create it."

It seems like a startlingly simple philosophy from someone who has built three Fortune 100 companies, developed the entire digital marketing campaign for Shakira, and produced one of the best independent films in recent memory (*Bella*). Despite the glamour of living in Cher's former home, and spending weekends with people like Roger Federer, Alec Baldwin, and P Diddy, Sean stays grounded by embracing his family's long tradition of hard-won wisdom.

The road to progress is paved with sacrifice. And your life philosophy is like a computer's operating system. It either helps you run more effectively and more efficiently from having good input, or in the case of people who try to get rewards before the sacrifice—it can be the equivalent of a virus. All of success in life comes down to a test of whether or not you will make a sacrifice when no one else is watching. Will you do it when no one will applaud you, or even notice you? Successful people do the right thing just because it's the right thing; that's integrity. And I think that the integrity of seeing it, speaking it, and then doing it builds an internal architecture that strengthens you.

As we were talking, a bottle of water fell on the floor.

See! All of life comes down to this simple choice! If you ignore that bottle of water and leave it for the staff to pick up, then it drains your integrity fuel tank. But if you stop and run back and pick it up and throw it out, something special happens: You earn a private victory *that fuels your tank. Ignoring it is energy draining, while picking it up is energy gaining. I don't know why that is the way it is; I just know that it's* definitely *the way it is.*

Making sacrifices also makes the taste of success so much more visceral. A drop of water to the man who stumbled across the finish line of a marathon tastes so much sweeter than a liter of soda to the man who quit before he was finished. Following through is always rewarded—sooner or later.

When you do right, you feel right. When you feel right, you think clearly. When you do wrong, you feel wrong, and when you feel wrong, you think cloudy. And once you have clouds of shame, anxiety, and/or fear, your environment becomes a fertile ground for an unethical lifestyle, which will produce more of the same. It is the small private failures during seemingly insignificant opportunities that lead to the surprising destruction of most people. Likewise, it is the small private victories that ultimately add up to their greatness.

When I stand up and throw the bottle away, I am at peace because I know I'm doing the right thing; and that one minuscule decision is representative of the tremendous life and business success that comes to those who reiterate that type of decision over and over again. First you see it, then you speak it, and then you have to do it. I believe that it is the small decisions that are enormous.

Go Create

Remember that when used with integrity, there is almost nothing more powerful than your own word. Words are the first manifestation of ideas or thoughts into the *real* world. At their origin, those ideas exist only in your mind, but once they have been spoken or written, then they *exist* and have the power to shape the world around us. The moment we galvanize our thoughts into *words* marks the onset of creation.

> Words are the first manifestation of ideas or thoughts into the *real* world.

Unfortunately, we don't recognize the simplicity of initiating the creation process and so we often don't place appropriate value on the use of our words. Here is a checklist of seven basic guidelines for preserving and harnessing the power of your word.

1. Think before you speak.
2. Choose your words carefully.

3. Do what you say you will.

4. Be where you promise you will.

5. Resist the urge to use emotionally charged, untamed language.

6. Assume the "mic is always on" and that everyone will hear everything you say.

7. Use empowering language when speaking about yourself and others.

Integrity is one of the only things that you take with you everywhere you go. You are in charge of creating the world around you.

You think it, you speak it, you act, it happens.

Now all you have to do is find a way to fit it all in . . .

For more ideas on how to manifest your dreams into reality, follow Rory on Twitter at www.roryontwitter .com.

5

SCHEDULE

THE HARVEST PRINCIPLE

armers have a harvest each and every year. It's one period of the year when all of their crops must be taken up at just the right time in order for their survival. Do you know how many hours the average farmer works per day during harvest season?

About eighteen.

They usually wake up around 4:30 a.m. and come in around 11 p.m. Given the fact that their entire livelihood and well-being over the next year are dependent on the fruits of this harvest season, do you think that taking a sick day is an option?

Do you think that being tired is an option for the farmer? Do you think that taking time off to "evaluate other career options" is a possibility for a farmer during harvest?

Absolutely not. There is a short window of opportunity when the harvest must be captured. It doesn't matter if the farmer would rather work eighteen hours a day at some other time of the year because the harvest is when the harvest is.

Feeling fatigued, burnt out, or dissatisfied doesn't enter into a farmer's decision-making framework during the harvest because that is the only time of the year that will produce the type of results needed to make life work.

Instead of evaluating, in the "heat of the moment," whether or not he feels like working, the farmer instead sets up his life in a way that allows him to prepare for the coming harvesttime so as to maximize the reap. Whether or not you've ever stepped foot on a farm, the law of the harvest is one you need to become intimately acquainted with if you are committed to a Take the Stairs mind-set. The law of the harvest says: Focused effort is amplified by appropriate timing and regimented routine.

> Focused effort is amplified by appropriate timing and regimented routine.

Why are we talking about farming? Because within this law of the harvest lies the best available solution to the modern world's number one problem: time.

The Myths of Time Management

Time management is the number one reason people get into our coaching program, and it seems to be the number one problem that individuals, families, companies, and entrepreneurs all share.

With an infinite number of options vying for our attention, just deciding how best to spend our time and fit everything in is a major cause of stress today. The simple Take the Stairs solution to the problem is not doing everything that we *can* do in a day, but rather to do everything we *should* do in a day. Unfortunately, we've been led astray by popular misconceptions about time that don't serve us well. First and foremost, the myth of *balance*.

We hear the word "balance" all the time these days, particularly in the all-too-commonplace phrase "work-life balance." Many of us think of balance as dividing our time equally among equal activities because, by definition, "balance" means equal distribution in opposite directions. But if you take a step back and consider this for a moment, you'll see that it's an impossible

> Balance shouldn't mean equal time spent on equal activities. Balance should mean appropriate time spent on critical priorities.

and dubious goal as it relates to how we spend our time. It's also a somewhat useless strategy for managing time because some activities simply don't require as much time as others.

For example, being in great physical shape can be accomplished in 30 minutes on just three days a week. There is no need to spend the same amount of time in that area of your life as in the amount it takes to complete your work, for example. Balance shouldn't mean equal time spent on equal activities. Balance should mean appropriate time spent on critical priorities.

Not "Enough," But "When"

The biggest problem with the notion of balance is that it causes us to ask the wrong questions. Instead of asking, "Am I spending *enough* time on this activity?" we should really be asking, "*When* is the best time to be focused on this activity?"

Achieving balance is not only a questionable goal; it's also an impossible one. The world we live in is constantly changing, and therefore requires a more nuanced approach. Life's tragedies and triumphs, tasks and trivialities seem to follow ebb and flow of up and down, more and less. Life, like nature, operates in seasonal periods of intensity and decline much more like a harvest. This is where the farmer's law of harvest comes in.

There are all kinds of seasons in life. We have seasons of

education, seasons of independence, seasons of love, seasons of growth, seasons of new beginnings, seasons of sickness, and seasons of health. A "season" as I am describing it here could be as long as a few years or as short as a few minutes. Much of the anxiety I've noticed in the lives of our coaching clients is due to the fact that they are trying to take on too many seasons at once, and some of them are naturally conflicting.

We need to be more intentional in planning and aligning our seasons in a realistic fashion. For example, if you are in a season of having a baby, it's probably not a good time to start a season of entrepreneurship. If you're in a season of heavy work-load, it's not a good time to start a season of remodeling your home.

Instead of asking ourselves, "How can I fit *more* in?" we should be asking, "What season(s) is my life in *right* now, when is the *right* time to be completing its associated activities, and what are the *right* things I need to do to maximize my harvest of this season?" Focused effort is amplified by appropriate timing and regimented routine.

CPAs, athletes, newlyweds, salespeople, schools, parents, and even nature all have seasons. With each season comes a set of laws and circumstances that govern that season—our task is to work within those guidelines to create the best outcomes possible. When we are aware of the season we are in and focused on maximizing the results of that season, we have natural clarity about our priorities, and as a by-product we get amplified synergy of our results. Yet as we ignore the inevitability of the laws of these seasons, we frustrate ourselves by trying to harvest results at *inappropriate* times with *inappropriate* activities and an *inappropriate* focus on too many things at one time.

If you were going to go fishing, when would you go? You go early in the morning or you go at dusk in the evening. Why? Because that's when the fish are biting. You could go fishing at 11 a.m., and cast as many lines into the water as you want—that is, work as hard as you can and as fast as you can—but you simply won't get the same results as you would with that same amount of energy applied in the morning or in the evening. The proper question, again, is not necessarily, "Am I fishing the right amount of time?" but, "Am I fishing at the right time?"

You might already take this approach when it comes to fishing, but most of us don't apply it to our work and family life. Instead of asking, "How much can I get done today?" we should be asking, "What is the most effective thing I can be doing right now with the time I have available?" This small shift can yield massive results.

Double-Time Part Time for Full-Time Free Time

From our discussion of the Magnification Principle of Focus, we know that focus is power. Combine focus with timing, and you truly have a winning combination. Focused work in the season of the harvest, when the soil is ready and the conditions are right, will always yield more than the same amount of work (or more) when the conditions aren't right.

In other words, the Take the Stairs mind-set is not about hard work, or smart work; it's about both.

The amazing thing about focusing our work at the most advantageous time is that we can get things done much faster than we otherwise would. At Southwestern we call this phenomenon "Double-Time Part Time for Full-Time Free Time (DTPTFTFT)." In other words, the Take the Stairs approach says I'll work double-time part time now (at the appropriate time and season) for full-time free time later.

> The Take the Stairs mind-set is not about hard work, or smart work; it's about both.

What is amazing about the "Double-Time Part Time Full-Time Free Time" mentality is how dramatically different and better the results are in each of the areas of our life. For example, if you are in a season of getting out of debt, you have to work. You have to fight. You have to push. You have to go all out with everything you've got to make every single extra penny you can while saving what you've got to the extreme.

Dave Ramsey lays out a debt reduction program in *Total Money Makeover*, and he says that it takes the average person in the program eighteen to thirty-six months to get out of debt. When I first learned about this book, I had over $45,000 of debt, but I hammered away at it. I got on a budget schedule saving every single penny, working constantly overtime, making extra sales calls, pushing it to the absolute max stressing over every single little penny until one day, two years later, I looked up and I was FREE!

For the rest of my life I will be free. For the rest of my life I can go out to eat all I want, buy anything I want, and do anything I want as long as I can pay with cash because I am full-time free! But I probably would've never got there if I just worked normal hours, with normal focus, and normal intensity. It had to be extra intense for a short period of time; it had to be treated like a harvest season.

Here's another example from my own experience. In 2003, I weighed 215 pounds. I ate fast food every day, lived on soda, and hated running. I decided in one moment that I was going to stop eating fast food completely, 100% eradicate carbonated beverages from my diet, and get on a new eating schedule. I also decided I was going to run for 30 minutes every single day on a new highly intensified workout schedule until my life changed. I worked out late at night or early in the morning if I had to, I focused on every single thing that went into my body, I maxed it out every day at the gym. I worked double-time part time until one day eight months later I got on a scale and had lost 40 pounds.

Now I have dessert when I want, I work out only a couple times a week, and even occasionally have fast food but I can because I'm full-time free. Of course, full-time free doesn't mean that you never have to work again; it just means that when you apply extreme discipline for a defined period of time (a "season"), you create freedom from the stress and worry that comes from typical performance. Double-time part time sets your life up in a way that you make sacrifices for the short term to create a long term that is much more manageable.

Freedom in any area of your life is available to you if you're willing to focus in on a relevant season one by one working double-time part time for full-time free time.

> Discipline creates freedom.
> —Randy Gage

Needless to say, I did not take on these projects all at once. Getting out of debt and getting in shape were tackled in different seasons. To quote my pal Randy Gage, "Discipline creates freedom," but timing is everything.

Applying DTPTFTFT to Your Daily Life

After studying thousands of successful people and working with them closely in our coaching program, it seems that they simply do what they have to do when they have to do it and they pay the price in the short term so that they can reap the benefits in the long term (the Paradox Principle of Sacrifice).

Part of why so many companies and families are falling apart in today's escalator environment is that we want the results and the full-time free time without first being willing to put in the double-time part time. We have to pay the price for success in any endeavor, and according to the Harvest Principle of Schedule, it almost always comes precisely through IMBALANCE!

A healthy approach to time management in the twenty-first century is one that asks, "Is what I'm doing right now the best use of my time at this moment? Am I accomplishing the most important item at the most opportune time?"

Instead of trying to do a lot of things equally at once for the sake of doing a little bit of everything, it is better to be selecting one or a few of the most critical priorities and effectively imbalancing your life in the direction of the most timely. Of course, what is timely and what is most important are constantly shuffling and changing according to each of the areas of our daily lives.

"On Schedule" Is a Mind-Set

A big part of a Take the Stairs mind-set is staying "on schedule." This means more than just being where you're supposed to be, doing what you're supposed to be doing, when you're supposed to be doing it. "On schedule" is a mind-set. It's a condition of mental toughness.

We are lucky that one of the greatest salesmen on the planet, Dave Brown, just so happens to be one of our partners at Southwestern Consulting. Dave was making as much as $19,000 per month in his midtwenties purely from having made more than 35,000 cold calls (door-to-door and over the phone). Many would call Dave a master salesman, and while it's true that Dave has broken just about every sales record for anything he's ever been involved with, he says that his extraordinary production is more a function of his commitment to staying on a regimented routine. "I have a goal and I have a plan that I know will take me to the destination I want. It is broken down to exactly what I need to be doing every second of every day, and I'm irrevocably committed to working according to that plan. The results always just seem to take care of themselves."

For you today, in your life and in your business, isn't it true that sometimes you feel "on schedule" and sometimes you feel "off schedule"? When you are "on schedule," things are working, you are working, and you are fervently moving toward your vision of success.

Being on schedule means having a regimented routine *within* a harvest season. One of the biggest ways we lose time and energy is thinking about where we have to go next. Having a schedule eliminates that issue and it provides a structured regimen that allows us to focus our energy on the tasks at hand. Instead of asking over and over, "What should I be doing now?" you are well on your way to getting it done.

Rocks, Pebbles, Sand

A professor once had a glass jar sitting at the front of his class with large rocks in it up to the top. He asked the students, "Is this jar full?" To which they all replied, "Yes, of course it is." The professor then took a handful of pebbles from behind his desk and dropped them into the jar, where they settled in around the rocks. He then asked, "Is the jar full *now*?" And then with a smile they said, "Okay, *now* it's full."

From behind his desk the professor then pulled a cup of sand, which he proceeded to pour into the jar, watching as it filled in comfortably around both the rocks and the pebbles. He then asked once more, "Class, is this jar full?" Now realizing that it couldn't possibly be filled any further because there was no visible space, they said, "Okay, *now* it is definitely full."

Yet again from behind his desk the professor pulled out another element. This time it was a pitcher of water, and as he poured it in, it filled in the last remaining space in the jar. He then turned to the class and said, "As in life, we often think we can do no more, but when we push to be creative, we find that there is always room for us to fill."

That story is probably one of the oldest in the personal development world, but I've never heard a better metaphor for creating an effective schedule. So many people live with the excuse "I don't have time." They let that be the reason they can't be a great husband or wife, mom or dad, business owner or employee.

That is probably the single most cited excuse that we use as to why we don't achieve our dreams.

Don't allow yourself the indulgence of saying, "I'm too busy" or "I don't have time." It's an indulgence because as soon as you say, "I'm too busy," your creativity disengages and you are suddenly "off the hook." I'm not saying that you aren't busy— in fact, let's just assume you are busy. You are probably so busy that you don't know how you could possibly fit any-

> Don't allow yourself the indulgence of saying, "I'm too busy."

thing else in—but that's exactly the point. The moment you tell yourself you're too busy is the moment you stop thinking creatively about how to get other potentially important items into your schedule and your routine.

So often we think that we can either have time or have money. We think we can either be professionally successful *or* have a great family life. We think we can either have fun *or* save money. One of the most powerful wealth files from *Secrets of the Millionaire Mind* by T. Harv Eker is that rich people always think in terms of "both." They continue to question and be creative to find a way while others simply accept what seems obvious. They see the jar as mostly full and they stop there.

I've always been amazed at how the most successful people I know are involved in so many things. They have so many friends, wonderful families, successful businesses, generous philanthropy, meaningful spiritual lives, healthy financial lives, and active physical lives.

These people understand the message of the rocks, pebbles, sand story. They learn to become comfortable with being uncomfortable, and they find a way to "fit it all in" and "make it all work" by understanding the order and timing in which those items are placed. What other people use as an excuse they see as a challenge—one they take joy and pride in rising above.

DON'T WASTE A SECOND

Case Study: Chad Goldwasser, Real Estate, Austin, Texas

One of my favorite examples of a person who is able to "fit it all in" is a coaching client of ours named Chad Goldwasser. When we first met, Chad was thirty-six years old, had three kids, was in peak physical condition, had amazing relationships, and all of his friends had the nicest things to say about him. Not only that but he was able to orchestrate social events for his community and to perform huge fund-raisers each year for very worthwhile causes. He was active in his church, savvy with his money, and passionate in every area of life. Oh, and I forgot to mention that his team sold 543 homes that year and he was the former number one Keller Williams Real Estate Agent in the world out of over 72,000 agents!

One night over dinner I asked him in detail about his schedule. It was incredible! He had every single minute of every single day Monday through Saturday exactly planned out, from first waking up, until hitting the pillow at an exact time. The part that was unique about it was that Chad had entire large blocks of time dedicated to his most important priorities. It was like he had "mini-harvest seasons" inside of a week—or even a day.

For example, every Tuesday night Chad dedicated fully to work. In his case, he was making prospecting calls for nearly three straight hours. He never stopped to check email, never stopped to eat, and barely stopped to go to the bathroom. Every Wednesday night, Chad and his wife had a dedicated date night—just the two of them investing time in their marriage. He didn't interrupt it by working on business, he didn't interrupt it by taking calls from other friends, and he didn't let the kids' activities encroach on that precious time with his spouse.

On Monday, Wednesday, and Friday mornings Chad worked out for short but intense periods. He found that he could remain in great shape by just hitting it hard in the gym three times a week.

He managed email by scheduling an appointment in his calendar—with himself! He treated email and office work like its own separate activity (rather than something to do all day here and there), and he didn't book other meetings during that time or take incoming calls. Likewise, he turned off his email notification window so that it didn't distract him from other things he might be working on. And anyone who knows anything about selling real estate knows that Saturday is an important day, yet

Chad worked so hard during his work times of the week that he dedicated every other Saturday to being with his family!

In all of these instances he capitalized on the power of uninterrupted focus. He was able to be free of the anxiety of things piling up or the worry of missing out on something because he could let them build up for a while knowing comfortably that he had a dedicated mini-harvest season somewhere else in his schedule to catch up. Plus, since he generally stuck to the same things at the same times (regimented routine), he was able to get in the habit of having the necessary tools and resources available for the task at hand, and it actually trained the people around him to respond with certain issues at certain times. Overall, Chad was able to achieve greater results in all areas of his life by imbalancing and fully dedicating his attention and energy to one thing for one short mini-harvest season during the day. In the midst of all of this, his favorite thing to say is, "It's a privilege, not a sacrifice, to pay the price for my dreams."

The Fundamental Five

One of the key reasons for having a schedule is to make sure we're satisfying all of our commitments while creating a life we love that is free of stress and full of fun. Interestingly enough, we began to notice that ultraperformers, the superwealthy, and extraordinarily happy people from many different backgrounds seem to follow

some of the same routine habits. All of them had protected
"harvest periods" in their week
that were dedicated to five
basic areas of their life: Faith,
Family, Fitness, Faculty (career),
and Finances.

> It's a privilege, not a sacrifice, to pay the price for my dreams.
> —*Chad Goldwasser*

Regardless of what industry they worked in, how old they were, or where they lived, these high achievers had activities planned that were immovable "rocks" in their schedule every week. *Faith* is in the center simply because those interviewed frequently described it as their most important, and because *Faith* is interrelated to all of the others by way of providing the

THE FUNDAMENTAL FIVE

appropriate perspective to make each of them work more powerfully (more on this in the next chapter).

One story that is easy to create in our own minds is that "we can either be successful in our career *or* we can have a happy family." Yet *Family* was another commonly cited priority of these highly successful people. Part of their passion in work came from maintaining the attitude that all of the work they do is in service of their family. And let's face it, in business what you don't get done today can be done tomorrow, but with family what doesn't get done today is gone forever.

Fun was the only area that most of them didn't seem to have a detailed plan for each week. Although all of these individuals would characterize their life as extremely *Fun*, it was as if *Fun* was a by-product of getting effective results in the other five areas.

> In business what you don't get done today can be done tomorrow, but with family what doesn't get done today is gone forever.

There were very similar and basic "rules" that they all seemed to follow. We've consolidated those rules into a list that we now refer to as the Fundamental Five:

1. **Faith.** Start each day with ten minutes of inspirational reading from the Bible or other source, and engage in church or another spiritual practice of fellowship at least once a week.

2. **Family.** Have one weeknight dedicated as a private date night with a spouse or a child—even if it can only happen with each person once a month (randomly, the most common day was Wednesday).

3. **Fitness.** Do some physical activity every day (like 30 push-ups and 100 sit-ups) and work out hard for 30 minutes a day three times per week.

4. **Faculty.** If necessary, have one uninterrupted night per week (or two during a highly intense predefined and pre-communicated harvest season) dedicated to work or a personal hobby.

5. **Finances.** Review all of your up-to-date financial account balances every Sunday night.

In every instance, the value of planned and protected weekly time, even if it was small, created better results than doing a little "here and there" of each one. The good news for you busy people is that just like a harvest, not all time is created equal. As it turns out, success in these five "rocks" in our life is almost always based on quality of time and not necessarily on quantity of time.

> Success in the most important areas of life is based on quality of time and not quantity of time.

Having a relentless Take the Stairs mind-set about accomplishing these five activities will take less than a total of ten hours per week, but will be tantamount in helping create a life you love.

For me personally, I've always noticed that if I am being disciplined about my time at church and my time at the gym, then everything else in my life seems to fall into place. So those have become the two biggest "rocks" in my schedule.

Creating Your Ideal Schedule

It's pretty clear that the number one challenge for most people today is *time*. Yet when we advise people to create a written schedule, the way of the "escalator world" is to throw up our hands and claim that it is futile because there is just no way we can perfectly plan for all of the unexpected occurrences in any given day.

> If you don't know what your ideal week looks like, you will never have one.

It may be true that it's unlikely for us to stick to a perfect schedule. But one thing we know for sure is that if you don't know what your ideal week looks like, you will never have one.

To create a schedule, all you need is a spreadsheet; that is your jar. Dr. Stephen Covey has taught for years to put the big "rocks" in first, so start by putting in your Fundamental Five and then insert the "pebbles" like sleep and work meetings around them. The "sand" of things like email catch-up and office time will fall in naturally. The "water" then is whatever is left— and that's all free to do whatever you want!

START KEEPING SCORE

Case Study: Ian Koniak, Business Office Products, Los Angeles, California

It's nothing new to hear that that which is monitored is improved, and that what you don't measure you can't manage. But it is usually only the few people with a Take the Stairs mind-set who actually track their results.

Ian Koniak was a younger salesperson the first time he came to one of Southwestern Consulting's large public "Success Starts Now!" events. At the time, he had been sales rep of the year three straight times and was one of the top producers in the nation for Ricoh business solutions. After being promoted to Director of Sales for the entire greater Los Angeles area, he grew revenues 34% in very short order. While his awards and accolades are fancy, his method for success isn't. In his own words:

With regards to my personal system for self-discipline, I keep a calendar in my closet, which I mark at the end of each day.

Here are my weekly goals:

- *Work: 50 hours/week*
- *Internet browsing and television (my time-stealers): No more than 7 hours/week*
- *Sleep: Average at least 7 hours/night*
- *Gym: 3 days/week*

At the end of each day, I will write how many hours I worked that day, how many hours I spent watching TV or surfing the web, how much sleep I got, and if I went to the gym. At the end of each week I total my hours in each category, and if I did not hit my weekly goal, I revise my following week's goals so that they would coincide with my ultimate target.

My goal for this system is to make sure I live a healthy lifestyle (sleep + exercise) and that I am working enough hours to be successful in my job (based on my years in this business, I know that I need to put in the required hours to hit my aggressive targets). I also want to make sure I am not wasting time browsing the web and watching too much TV.

If I don't track this daily and have accountability, I have no way of measuring my goals on a weekly basis. The system is very elementary, but it works great for me (I've been doing this for years).

The activities that Ian is tracking are what we at Southwestern refer to as a person's CSFs (Critical Success Factors). They vary for each person and each situation, but our experience working with clients has been that simply identifying and monitoring these critical factors can create as much as a 30% increase in productivity. If you're serious about reaching a goal, these critical factors will rise to a level of priority that is beyond the convenience of what your schedule normally allows for.

One of the biggest ways we lose time is by not knowing where we're going next. Having a schedule allows you to take the thought process out of much of which activities you should or shouldn't spend time on, because you've thought through them all at once in a logical state, rather than waiting until you're in the moment, emotionally deciding whether or not you *feel* like taking certain actions.

The payoff here is that you can finally let go of a lot of the worry and stress in your life if you simply create a well-designed schedule and commit to following it. If you do, then very quickly you will find your productivity increasing, and good work habits taking shape.

Creating an ideal schedule and keeping score is one early discussion we have with all of our coaching clients. It sometimes takes a bit of work to convince them to try it, but it often completely transforms their life and is largely responsible for their measurable results in the end. It will do the same for you, so get to it.

Preparing for the Inevitable

Vince Lombardi once said, "Winning is a habit; unfortunately, so is losing." He understood that the results we get in life are simply the by-product of our repeated effort and our regimented schedule.

Improving your self-discipline, then, happens not only from creating a good schedule but also from learning to recover from getting *off schedule*. Let's be honest, we all fall off the path from time to time. Sometimes it's not our fault, and sometimes it is—but sooner or later we're all going to get thrown for a loop.

Don't get me wrong; you've had great streaks before. Remember that time when you were going to the gym every day at 6 a.m.? Or that month when you were completely focused and relentlessly committed at work? But what happens? Either our motivation burns out, or an event occurs that throws us off schedule, and it becomes increasingly difficult to get back on track.

Prepare yourself for those setbacks in advance. No matter what schedule you're on or what goal you're pursuing, it is inevitable that your plan won't go perfectly. The solution to *off schedule* is to learn to shift your focus away from the results that aren't within your control.

Too many people get upset or discouraged because they focus on results that are not within their control. In other words, they let their sense of self-worth be defined by outcomes rather than effort, so that when they don't experience overnight success, or they get off track, they start to disregard their schedule. If you're in sales or business, you can't control who will buy from you; you can only influence it through good customer service, a high-quality product, and the number of people you talk to. If you're in a competition, you can't control for sure whether or not you will win; you can only influence it by practicing hard and executing a well-devised game plan.

> A Take the Stairs mind-set means knowing that today's work turns into next week's success.

Part of adopting the Take the Stairs mind-set is learning to take pride in controlling the activities that are *within your power* and to let go of the worry and fear attached to the results that are not. A Take the Stairs mind-set means knowing that today's work turns into next week's success.

Schedule and the Slinky Effect

Do you remember the Slinky—that toy that was really nothing more than a metal wire wrapped into the shape of a cylinder?

I used to love those things. Of course, the best part about a Slinky was dropping it down the stairs and watching it fall over itself all the way to the bottom.

A slinky is the best metaphor I can think of for the relationship between your schedule and your results. Working a defined schedule is an investment and it is what you lead with; but results of that labor usually tail behind it with delayed manifestation. Part of the Take the Stairs mind-set is understanding that you always get paid for how hard you work, but it's not always right away.

> You always get paid for how hard you work, but it's not always right away.

Your schedule works like a Slinky because the efforts you make create the energy—they lead the way—and the results follow, at some times more slowly than at others. There is a gap between the work you put in from being on schedule and when the results start to show up.

That delay in seeing results explains why people often have a hard time sticking to their schedule. Our natural instinct is to want to see the fruits of our labor right away and to see the return on our investment immediately. But that's not how discipline works, and it's not how your schedule works.

As Dave Ramsey says, "Discipline is not a microwave; it's a Crock-Pot." It does work, and it is better for you, and it has greater impacts on your life but it often takes awhile. Having that perspective has everything to do with managing your own *off schedule.*

I also love the Slinky image because we all know that sense of momentum and rhythm that simple toy can have when it's "doing its thing," descending the stairs as if on its own. Of course, it was your initial placement that set it in motion. It's the same thing with being on a great schedule. Everything seems to be in place and we start to feel "on a roll." We put in work, we are focused, our attitude is great, and naturally the results are coming. Success breeds success, and it's easy to keep the momentum going.

But the moment that something interrupts our schedule (maybe an unexpected setback, life event, or just taking our eye off the ball), we lose our focus, our rhythm, and our momentum. The Slinky comes to a slamming stop right on top of itself.

So what do you do to get yourself out of this predicament? Simple: Get relentless about putting your self-esteem into your work habits instead of your results.

This makes it much easier to get back on track. You simply have to get that positive momentum going again. *You* set it in motion before, and *you* can do it again. Stay focused on initiating a harvest season of work habits. Once you get it going, that momentum will carry you forward, and the results are sure

> Get relentless about putting your self-esteem into your work habits instead of your results.

to follow. After all, the Slinky doesn't go down the stairs on its own; it requires someone—you—to set it in motion.

If even during those times when you're *off schedule* you can maintain the right mind-set and recommit to getting back on track, winning will inevitably follow. It's all a matter of your perspective . . .

For free tips on time management, subscribe to Rory's YouTube channel at www.roryonyoutube.com.

6

FAITH

THE PERSPECTIVE PRINCIPLE

n the movie *Dead Poets Society*, Robin Williams stands on top of a desk in a classroom and says, "I stand on this desk to remind myself that we must constantly look at things in a different way." There may not be a more relevant statement to improving our self-discipline than that. To change your behavior, change your perspective.

Tape Measure Timeline

I once had the good fortune of listening to a guest speaker who is one of the world's most renowned motivators and youth experts, Eric Chester. Eric performed a physical demonstration that has permanently etched itself into my memory and into my life philosophy on perspective.

Eric had two student volunteers come up from out of the audience. One of them he handed the silver tab on the end of a very long tape measure marking "0 feet." He then asked the other student to grab the handle of the tape measure and walk it out exactly 80 feet, nearly all the way around the room.

"The average male life span is about eighty years," said Eric. "Since there are twelve inches in a foot and there are twelve months in a year, then each foot on this tape measure represents one year of your life. And each inch on this tape measure represents one month of your life. So here now, stretched out in front of you, is the appropriate to-scale view of your entire life."

Chester went on to explain that our four years in college (represented by feet "18–22") was the time of our life that we were in at that time. He said that if you take out the time that we are sleeping during those four years, and the time we weren't actually in class or studying (a total of about 16 hours a day or two-thirds of that entire time), and account for the summer breaks, then this seemingly long time in college was just over a mere 1 foot out of our 80-foot timeline.

Yet he showed us how making good choices and working incredibly hard for those tiny 12 inches could set us up for an entire lifetime, some next 60 years (60 feet), of success. Likewise, making one wrong decision, in one moment, on one day would also set our life on an entirely different trajectory for a very long time.

According to Eric's tape measure timeline, a "bad day" wasn't even visible. It was approximately one-thirtieth of one inch.

With enough perspective, all of our failures—and successes—are reduced to their appropriate size. Every day our frustrations are so big, our losses are so big, and our problems are so big; if we view them only with the limited perspective of how it affected our day. But when you look at your life with the perspective of the entire 80 feet, the challenges of today are often a speck of unnoticeable dust on the timeline of our life.

How much greater is your perspective if you look at your life in the context of all of recorded history, which would be thousands and thousands of feet of tape measure? How much greater yet still is your perspective if you look at it through the lens of eternity?

If we have enough faith to believe that there is a future coming and we make appropriate account of it, then we would also have a basis for a more appropriate perspective relating to today's issues and today's struggles. When we lose faith in the future and we lose focus of where today fits into the greater timeline of the history of our lives, then we have no basis for perspective. The size of today's challenges is measured only against the shortness of today.

Faith can take many forms. It can mean faith in God, or some other higher power. It doesn't matter what you call it, or if you even give it a name at all. Having it means the difference between constantly worrying about the present and having the peace of knowing that you will transcend life's day-to-day setbacks in the long run.

The extent of our faith determines the term of our perspective, and the term of our perspective determines the size of our problems.

A challenge in respect to today is a big problem.

A challenge in respect to our life span is a small problem.

A challenge in respect to eternity is no problem.

Having this faith, this long-term perspective, enables us to make better decisions. It gives us the strength to endure short-term sacrifices. It empowers you with the conviction of knowing that things will work out for the better if you put in the work.

You can't make the hard right decisions today without faith in tomorrow. Why would you eat healthy food if you didn't believe it would actually make you healthy? Why would you work out if you didn't believe it would actually make you look and feel better? Why wouldn't you charge your credit card into oblivion if you felt there would be no price to pay in the end?

> Sometimes we make choices not out of a lack of discipline, but out of a lack of perspective and faith.

You see, sometimes we make choices not out of a lack of discipline, but out of a lack of perspective and faith. Yet with limited perspective, we make decisions that lead to pain. With limited perspective, we have no explanation of tragedy.

Broadening our perspective, taking a step back to look at the entire tape measure of our lives, empowers us to make decisions that will make us happier in the long run. It shrinks our momentary ups and downs to their appropriate size. It provides an explanation for setbacks and even tragedies. Broadening our perspective allows us to have peace of mind.

That's the Perspective Principle of Faith: Our ability to have peace is directly proportionate to the term of our perspective.

Eric Chester's tape measure timeline is the single most powerful display of this principle that I've ever seen. It made an instant mark on my life and immediately empowered me to make decisions that other people around me weren't making. Not because I wanted to choose the difficult right over the easy wrong, not because I was somehow special, and not because I was weirdly addicted to masochistic behavior.

It empowered me because I had a longer-term perspective that enabled me to see toward a greater future and take interest in that future rather than the natural human tendency to take interest only in what was right in front of me. I call that perspective "faith." It was at that moment I decided to put my faith and hope into enjoyable results more than enjoyable processes.

For you in your life, especially if you are having difficulty making the short-term decisions you want to make, change your perspective. Step back and look at choices through the lens of

> Put your faith into enjoyable results instead of enjoyable processes.

the whole tape measure of your life and not just what's right in front of you today.

Think about this for a minute. Can't you look back at some point in your life when something turned out terribly different from the way you had planned, but now looking back, you can absolutely say it happened for the best? Of course!

It might have been a relationship or a job that fell apart that totally destroyed you emotionally at the time and you couldn't understand why it was happening the way that it was, but looking back now, you can see *exactly* why it happened that way. And you're probably thankful for it!

But at the time, in that moment you were frustrated because you didn't have the benefit of perspective. In fact, frustration shows up only in the absence of perspective. Taking a longer view can make all the difference.

Seeing the World Through the Barrel of a Pen

The escalator mind-set all around us is relentlessly focused on the here and now. Are we happy right now? Are we comfortable right now? Are things going our way right this minute? If not, let's quit what we're doing and find something that feels better.

People who have mastered self-discipline take a more long-term perspective. Whether their here and now is filled with pain or triumph, they gain peace from adopting an attitude of "do your best and forget the rest." They know that if they work hard and do everything in their power, then sooner or later things will work out, even if they haven't just yet.

I've noticed that almost always in my life when I'm frustrated, depressed, or disappointed, my perspective has been reduced to the here and now. To help me see the bigger picture, I developed a silly physical reminder that I pull out whenever I'm discouraged. I simply hold my pen up to my eye and stare directly down its barrel. But then I pull the pen away from my eye and look at it in its entirety, and it reminds me that I need to look at my life the same way. I need to recalibrate my perspective in order to find peace. It's an everyday reminder that

THE CONTEXT TEST

Narrow Scope:
Focusing on the
here and now

Broad Scope:
Considering the
bigger picture

in those moments I'm looking at my life with limited context; I'm not looking at the whole tape measure; I'm not looking with appropriate perspective.

Doing this also makes me smile because it reminds me how goofy I can be—and that is a perspective we all need sometimes.

Becoming the World's Number One Loser

As I've mentioned, Toastmasters International has made a significant impact on my life. Toastmasters is a nonprofit organization dedicated to improving its members' public speaking, communication, and leadership skills through local weekly meetings and a mostly volunteer leadership structure. With more than 260,000 members in more than 100 countries, it is comprised of some of the most encouraging and uplifting people in the world—and I'm a proud product of the organization.

Shortly after I joined Toastmasters, I met a man named Ed Tate, who had the title of the World Champion of Public Speaking. Wow! This guy apparently had entered a contest that Toastmasters International holds each year in which 30,000 contestants compete over the course of nine months for a chance to be called World Champion.

Long story short, I set a goal of competing in this contest. I read, networked, practiced, and practiced some more. I cold-called high schools, churches, chambers of commerce, Kiwanis clubs, Rotary clubs, comedy clubs, Lions clubs, Key clubs, and Toastmasters clubs begging for them to give me what my mentor and 2001 World Champ Darren LaCroix kept telling me I needed: "Stage time, stage time, stage time!" I would drive an hour and a half each way down to Colorado Springs for five minutes in front of an audience in the back room of a Denny's restaurant! It consumed my every waking minute.

A year later, I made it to the World Championship of Public Speaking. I was in the top ten speakers in the world—and lost. The year after that, I came back even stronger, worked harder, studied more, and got even more stage time. All told, I gave 304 free speeches and made it back to the World Championship.

My entire family, our closest friends, and our whole team from Southwestern Consulting was in the audience of thousands of people. All of my preparation had been completed, and innumerable hours and dollars had been invested in this one moment. I went out and delivered the absolute best speech of my life, giving every single thing I had . . . and I came in second.

Despite my cordial smile on stage when I heard the results, I was crushed. Mentally devastated. Emotionally discouraged. Physically deflated. I could barely breathe and choked back the tears as everything I had worked for all coalesced into this one moment of defeat. I didn't understand how something I had worked so hard for—something I cared so deeply about—could have ended this way. You might be thinking, "Gee, second place isn't so bad," but to me, in that moment, it was a crushing defeat.

Later that evening I realized something, though. *I had given it my all. There was nothing more I could have done.* And at that exact moment I felt the pain of disappointment dissolving into peace because I realized I wasn't in control. *I* had done everything in *my* power. I had done every single little tiny possibly imaginable thing that I could think of to win—and I didn't.

Do you see the beauty in that? *I* had done everything I could. So I *knew for sure* it wasn't my fault. There was no way that I had done anything wrong because there was nothing that I left out and nothing I would've done differently. While it didn't make me a champion, I did know for sure that I had nothing to regret. I could now accept the outcome and try to learn from it moving forward.

Therein lies the gargantuan payoff of self-discipline and faith. When you do everything that you can, and all that is in your power, and things still don't work out the way you had hoped or planned, then you can be *absolutely sure* that they were *definitely supposed* to go the way they did. There is nothing more you could have done.

People without discipline and without faith don't get that same payoff of peace. If you didn't have enough faith that things would work out for the better to even get started, or if you didn't have the discipline to do everything in your power to make them happen, then you know, deep down, why the results turned out the way they did. You didn't do every-thing you could have. You

> A true champion has character and class regardless of circumstances.

can't be sure if you are living the life you are destined for unless you are doing every single thing in your power to make your life better. But if you are doing everything in your power, then you can have faith that things went exactly as they were *supposed to*. Having faith like that is extraordinary, and that is why a true champion always has character and class regardless of circum-stances.

Dead Level Best

One of my all-time favorite movies is *Facing the Giants*. It's about a high school football team struggling to find and implement faith into their lives and their sport. One scene, in particular, is my absolute favorite.

A young player named Brock is asked to do the death crawl on all fours across the football field for a second time, except this time his coach challenges him to give his absolute best.

Brock first suggests that he can go to the 30-yard line. The coach suggests the 50, with another player on his back . . . blindfolded.

The coach says that he doesn't care how far Brock goes as long as he gives his very best. His absolute best. In dramatic style, Brock pushes himself to the limit and collapses when he's done. He takes off the blindfold to see that he's at . . . the opposite goal line 100 yards away. (Yes, I'm a sucker for motivational movie scenes.)

When it comes to a Take the Stairs mind-set, just about the only thing that matters is that we're doing our dead level best. Our absolute best. That we are giving everything we have in pursuit of a vision that we have decided is worthy of that much commitment and focus.

If you are really doing your best, then take pride in it, be excited about it, and keep it rolling! You are among an elite few who do their best every day, and because of your hard work— doing the things most people aren't willing to do—things will *absolutely* work out to be successful in your favor.

If you are not doing your best, if you are not doing every single little thing you know how to do, if you are not working with maximum intensity, then get your butt moving. You are not doing yourself any favors by meandering. You are allowing your dreams to fall victim to your inaction. You are trading what you want most for what you want *right now*. Most of all, you're denying yourself the rich rewards of hard-won success.

PLAYING MY PART

**Case Study: Tim Knight, Executive Search,
Nashville, Tennessee**

The Pinnacle Society is a consortium of the top seventy-five recruiting, placement, and search consultants each year from across the entire nation. Requiring a minimum of five years of experience and well over $300,000 in personal production each year, it is a collection of the truly elite performers in the industry. Tim Knight of SBR Executive Search has been a member of Pinnacle for nine consecutive years—that is, every year he has been eligible. Tim is a master of productivity.

Even as we were interviewing him, he was pacing around in his office talking to us on the phone. Tim works at a standing desk; he doesn't have a chair. He says that his resolute commitment to taking action, being efficient, and producing at a high level actually comes from a very connected faith.

I've always had great faith that if I do my best, then things will work out exactly as they are supposed to. Perhaps a difference between me and most people, however, is that I believe that faith is not just sitting around waiting for God to make things happen. Instead, I believe the prerequisite for getting results is that I must first do my part.

I know that when I take action on the most critical tasks of my day, first thing in the morning, that I'm demonstrating a faith that those things really are the most important and they'll contribute to the kind of success I want to have. Conquering the most challenging calls or to-do items first also gives me a confidence that carries me the rest of my day. I always know that the other items will either take care of themselves or still be there for me to deal with later. It's an interesting phenomenon, too, that luck always seems to follow the momentum of my disciplined hard work.

Tim also puts faith into simple and timeless principles of success.

Positive self-talk is critical, I work in blocks of time, and when I'm on the phone, I'm disconnected from the Internet, including email. So many people follow a line of thinking that if someone emails us, we have to get right back to them; it's not true. Plus, I check emails in the morning, midday, and in the evening, and there are very few things that can't wait four hours. We're not talking about waiting two weeks; we're talking about four hours.

Overall, I put my faith in important actions because I believe that my work is a calling. God put me here for a reason, and it's not just to make money but to encourage and support others through my example and through my words. We all have times when we're not motivated, but those are just emotions, and I don't see what they have to do with me getting my job done and fulfilling my purpose. I need to do my best and work my plan. Whenever that happens, I start spending time with other people and somehow I become more excited and motivated. My faith hasn't let me down yet.

Handling Tragedy:
We Never Know How
the Story Goes

In 1969, a woman named Jane was set to be married to Dalton, Georgia's most eligible bachelor, a young man named John. Tragically, six months before their wedding, John was killed in an accident. As you might imagine, Jane was devastated by this horrific and senseless event.

However, a year later she met a man named Ronnie, fell in love with him, and married him. She and Ronnie had three beautiful kids and were a storybook family living in a small town, actively involved in the church and community, and running the family business.

In 1997, tragedy struck again as Jane, who had never smoked a cigarette in her life, was diagnosed with terminal lung cancer. A year later she died, leaving behind a family wondering *how?* and *why?* Particularly, her only daughter, Amanda, to whom she was very close, was sent into somewhat of a tailspin questioning *why* this would happen to her family.

As often is the case with tragedy, Amanda entered into a new era of her life, letting go of the once perfect childhood she had been living, and ventured down a slightly more provocative path. Her new behaviors landed her a new set of friends, one of whom was a local boy from the county school who was a smooth-talking ruckus maker who could make parents love him by day and get their kids into trouble by night.

His name was Dustin. Dustin and Amanda became great friends over the years, and while in college at the University of Tennessee, Dustin got recruited for a crazy summer job selling educational children's books door-to-door.

One year prior to that, a student from the University of Denver named Rory had also been recruited for the same summer job. Rory struggled intensely during the summer while selling. He often thought about quitting and constantly questioned why he was putting himself through such strife and rejection, and how this could possibly be helping him live a better life. He couldn't see beyond his immediate circumstances.

But Rory loved the person he became in the process (and the loot he made), so he decided to come back for another selling summer; this time as a recruiter, too. That year Dustin broke the company's sales record and at the same time Rory became one of the top recruiters in the company's history.

Meeting on incentive trips and speaking around the country together on behalf of their company, Dustin and Rory became good friends and dreamed of one day starting a sales consulting and motivational speaking company.

A few years later Dustin and I joined as cofounders of that company (Southwestern Consulting) with Gary Michels, a few other partners, and one other person whom Dustin had recruited, a young woman named Amanda. One year after that, Amanda and I started dating, and three years after that, I asked her father, Ronnie, if I could have his daughter's hand in marriage.

My wife, Amanda, is the single greatest gift in my life. She is the reason I celebrate life so vibrantly each day. She is the reason I do what I do, and she is the one who gave me the confidence to write the book that you are now holding.

I didn't understand at the time why I had to go through such strife and struggle knocking on doors. Amanda certainly didn't understand why she was faced with the enormous loss of her mother during her teenage years. And I'm pretty sure, at the time, Jane didn't understand how things would ever work out after losing her first fiancé. I'm not suggesting that one thing caused another—but if there is no accident in 1969, then it's possible that there would have been no Amanda. Which would have meant that there is no Amanda and Rory. And if there is no Amanda and Rory, then it is quite possible that you would not be holding this book in your hands right *now*.

We never know how the story is going to go. We don't have the luxury of knowing why things happen the way they do. And absent the ability to see into the future, we aren't entitled to evaluate the reasons *bad* things happen today. Faith, therefore, is also choosing to believe that all that is happening today—good or bad—is part of an ultimately greater plan.

> We aren't entitled to evaluate the reasons *bad* things happen today.

What I do know is that my story has led me to you. And your story has led you to me. What we choose to do from this point forward has everything to do with how faithful we are that things are going to get better in the future—if we commit to doing our absolute best.

For free daily reminders on how to maintain perspective, find Rory on Facebook at www.roryonfacebook .com.

7

ACTION

THE PENDULUM PRINCIPLE

A professor was explaining to his class something called the Law of the Pendulum. He said, "The Law of the Pendulum states that once a pendulum is released, it cannot return to a point higher than the point from which it was released. Do you understand this law?" The students said yes. The professor replied, "Well, do you believe it?" Again they said yes.

He then pulled from his pocket a small, but perfect, pendulum. He pulled the pendulum back, let it go and said, "Class, the Law of the Pendulum states that once a pendulum is released, it cannot return to a point higher than the point from which it was released. Do you understand this law?" They all said yes. He responded, "Well, do you believe it?" And again they all said yes.

Now there was this one particularly arrogant student who was up toward the front of the class who blurted out, "Duh, it's only obvious." So the professor invited this arrogant student to come up to the front of the class, and he accepted. On the very left side of the room there was a desk with a chair on top of it. And the professor asked the arrogant student to get up into the chair, and he did.

Then the professor walked over to the middle of the classroom, pulled back a large curtain, and suspended from the ceiling was an iron cable. At the bottom of it were three 45-pound weights. The professor had constructed a very large, and perfect, pendulum in the classroom. The professor grabbed the pendulum and he slowly walked it right up to where the weights were near the tip of the arrogant student's nose, and he said, "The Law of the Pendulum states that once any pendulum is released it cannot return to a point higher than the point from which it was released. Do you understand this law?" And the arrogant student said this time much more shakily, "Yes." To which the professor said, "Well, do you believe it?" Just then the professor let the pendulum go!

It swung across to the right side of the room and was starting to return right toward the student's nose. What do you think that arrogant student did?

That's right. I got the heck out of that chair as fast as I could! The pendulum then swung back and it didn't hit the wall. You see, on this day the professor wasn't teaching the class about the Law of the Pendulum; he was teaching the class about a different law, the Law of Action. And the Law of Action says that it does not matter what we *say* we believe; our real beliefs are revealed by how we *act*.

You can understand the Law of the Pendulum and not believe in it. You can understand everything that we've talked about in this book, but not believe in it. The only way that we will know if you believe in any of what you've read in this book is if it actually causes you to make different decisions and take different actions.

My first pastor, Rick Rusaw, always said, "Rory, if you want to know what a person believes in, just look at their calendar and their checkbook, because what they spend their time and their money on is what they believe in the most." And so right now you're nearing the end of this book and you've got a decision to make about what you are going to do differently. What actions are you going to take? What is it that you've known for a while that you should be doing that you don't want to do? What are you going to do about it?

Having a Take the Stairs mind-set means that you don't just recognize your inadequacies; you resolve them. You don't just identify changes you

> You don't just recognize your inadequacies; you resolve them.

need to make; you make them. Being a successful person *requires* that you take action.

INSPIRED ACTION

Case Study: Peter Ferré, Insurance, Wallowa, Oregon

For some people, action can be a fleeting pursuit, a by-product of fluctuating emotions. But for Peter Ferré, action is simply the congruent alignment of his vision and what needs to be done to achieve that vision. Over the last twelve years, Peter and his incredible team have managed to build Legacy Financial Services into a $50 million supplemental insurance brokerage with more than 100 agents . . . from scratch. At the core of Peter's philosophy is a straightforward formula that he's employed throughout his career to guarantee action and, inevitably, success.

Although he's managed and built a variety of different businesses over his twenty-seven-year professional career with lots of great teams supporting him, the common thread that runs through each of his businesses is that he has *never* had a year when one of the companies didn't grow. Peter's explanation for his extraordinary consistency is:

To simply run your business like a business. Many of the biggest problems people are facing in business—and the world—today are the result of people not making logical business decisions.

Sometimes we get caught up in doing what we think *needs to be done, or we make decisions based on what we* feel *like doing, and that never makes any sense because it's unrelated to what the business actually needs. Four times a year, at the beginning of each quarter, we look at the critical metrics, and we allow the business to dictate to us what needs to be done, not the other way around. As long as we're looking at the right numbers, they never lie. Knowing that, it quickly becomes obvious what the business needs, and that directs our activities for the upcoming quarter. Sometimes that means that I'm personally going to have to do things that I might not want to do.*

Whether or not I like what the numbers of the business are telling me or whether I would prefer to do something else is irrelevant. I've traded all that in for a deep-rooted personal conviction that if I'm doing an effective job, then the business should grow every year. Therefore, we try to always make decisions based on what the business is telling us empirically rather than what we are feeling emotionally.

Of course, nothing matters if you don't first have a vision for what you want your business and your life to look like. I've come to realize that developing a clear vision is a learned skill and habit that is critical for consistent and long-term success in anything we do. Not only that, but once a person develops the skill of creating a clear and meaningful vision, it is then crucial for them to connect that vision and purpose to the activities that need to be done each day to make it a reality. We have to get ourselves to understand the relevance that each minor activity we are doing today has in relation to reaching our goals.

I've made innumerable mistakes in my career, and yet my family and I have ended up right where we've always pictured we would. At forty-seven, I work only when I want to and live on a ranch where my kids can ride their horses for two miles and still be in their own back-yard. We didn't get to this point because we have some supreme ability to motivate ourselves. We got here because part of our vision has been to help the people around us realize what their visions are for their own lives and they have in turn lifted us up. For all of us, we know that when the connection between what we need to do and what we want to accomplish is clear and strong, it is not very difficult to take the actions necessary to make it happen. If the connection between what needs to be done and what one wants to accomplish is not strong, then it is going to be difficult for most anyone to wake up in the morning with a passion to tackle the challenges that consistent success requires.

Much of this book has been about your mind-set and the psychology of how to think differently. All of that thought and understanding is critical because the right mind-set precedes proper movement, but the bottom line of seeing change and results in your life is you need to ACT! You have to go and *do something*!

Wisdom is simply the application of knowledge and

> You are much more likely to act your way into healthy thinking than to think your way into healthy acting.
> —Roger Seip

the application of everything you've learned about in this book is manifested in one simple way: ACTION. You start doing the things you don't feel like doing. You set aside short-term discomfort for long-term results. You move. You act. You create motion. You cause change. You win.

I hope you will consider, absorb, debate, reflect on, and even adopt the principles I've presented here. But at the end of the day, that is meaningless if there is no action. As my friend Roger Seip once told me: "You are much more likely to *act* your way into healthy thinking than to *think* your way into healthy acting."

You'll notice that nowhere in this book did we talk about what you *should* do. That's because I don't think you need me or anyone else to tell you that. It's not my right. But even more important, I believe that most of us *already know* what we should do. The problem is that we don't do it. For most of us, it's not as much a matter of skill as it is a matter of will.

> The problem for most of us is not as much a matter of skill as it is a matter of will.

What We're Up Against: The Law of Diminishing Intent

Procrastination seductively destroys our dreams more than any other controllable force.

It robs us of our greatest passions and leaves nothing in its place except a wake of ultimately unfulfilling excuses. Therefore, we have to constantly be managing ourselves to take action against a dynamic enemy that is perpetually working against us.

The culprit I'm referring to is something called diminishing intent, and like so many saboteurs of our discipline, the biggest reason it is dangerous is because it is invisible. Most people set out on fire to achieve their goals because our intent to take action is strongest the moment we create that intention. Unfortunately, however, over time our initiative slowly starts to erode. The graph below illustrates the simple yet powerful effect of the Law of Diminishing Intent.

The classic example of this is the New Year's Resolution. If you go to the gym on January fifth at 6 p.m., what will you find? Of course, it's packed! There are people everywhere, lines for the treadmills, and lots of supplement purchases being rung up.

If you go to that same gym at the same time of the day but on March fifth, what will you see? Suddenly everyone has dis-

LAW OF DIMINISHING INTENT

appeared and it's mostly vacant. What happened to all the people who made New Year's Resolutions? Are they bad people? Are they liars? Are they weak-willed? No, absolutely not.

They are simply, through their own unawareness, victims of the law of diminishing intent. They are people who do not realize how fickle—and fleeting— our own intentions can be. Understanding this phenomenon explains why New Year's Resolutions rarely work. We can't make a resolution once a year and expect it to leverage us to action for that entire period of time. Instead, as Albert Gray wrote in 1940, "Any resolution that is made today must again be made tomorrow." And the next day, and the next day, and the next day (remember the Rent Axiom?).

> Any resolution that is made today must again be made tomorrow.
> —Albert Gray

Action is a strategy and a habit, but it's also a way of thinking. Being able to take action results from having the appropriate mind-set, and now that you know who the opponent is, you actually have a chance at winning.

What's Holding You Back? The Three Faces of Inaction

In our work with clients, we consistently find that people who are struggling with inaction or procrastination invariably have one of the following three deep-rooted attitudes:

- Fear: "I'm scared to do it."
- Entitlement: "I shouldn't have to do it."
- Perfectionism: "I won't try to do it if I can't do it right."

These all-too-common problems affect people across all professions, ages, and endeavors. You show me a person who is not achieving life at the level they want to be and I'll show you one of these diagnoses. The good news is that they don't need to hold us back.

FEAR

It's an oldie but a goodie: "FEAR stands for False Evidence Appearing Real." That is almost always what fear is. It's a fictional story written by our own minds.

Why do so many of us succumb to fear? Because it's more convenient and more comfortable for us to let our dreams disappear than to muster up the discipline and the work ethic to go out and transform them into reality. The payoff of fear is that we don't have to try, we don't have to work, and we don't have to challenge ourselves to test our limits. In other words, the escalator mind-set allows our fears to thrive so that work required to achieve our dreams doesn't have to. In contrast, the Take the Stairs mind-set demolishes our fears so that the only option is to work to make our dreams come true. Action is the cure for fear.

> Action is the cure for fear.

I once heard the true story of a woman who was trapped in a burning building on a very high floor. She had an intense fear of heights and also an intense fear of closed-in spaces, so when the fire alarm went off, she absolutely refused to follow her colleagues into the stairwell to evacuate to safety.

She could not handle the thought of going down the stairs being able to look down in the middle all the way to the bottom. And the thought of being trapped inside the enclosed stairwell was just too much to endure and so instead she made a conscious choice to hide under her desk and wait to die. She was willing to choose death over facing her fears.

Finally a fireman found her and began to drag her toward the stairs. She resisted him, kicking and screaming, "I'm scared! I don't want to because I'm scared!" He couldn't get her to go anywhere until he looked her in the eye and said, "That's okay, do it scared."

"Do it scared. Do it scared. It's okay to be scared; just do it scared." He repeated this in her ear all the way down eighty flights to safety. The phrase saved her life in a literal sense, but it also transformed her life emotionally. The catchphrase became her mantra, which enabled her to make better choices both large and small.

Don't you have times like that in your life—when you know what you *should* do, but you allow fear to hold you back?

It's okay to be scared—do it scared. It's okay to be unsure—do it unsure. It's okay to be uncomfortable—do it uncomfortable. Just get started where you are. That is the attitude of the most disciplined and successful people on the planet.

You are going to develop the habit of acting in the face of fear. You are going to create movement and momentum. You are going to get closer to your fear so that you can understand it and overcome it.

ENTITLEMENT

Even more than fear, the attitude of entitlement is a symptom of today's escalator mentality. So many of us are frustrated because somehow we believe that we are entitled to a life that is supposed to be easier. We want someone else to work the long hours for us, someone else to solve our problems, someone else to teach us, someone else to get us out of debt, someone else to pay for our retirement, someone else to take care of our kids, someone else to make us feel good about ourselves, someone else to give us what we want. These beliefs are so ingrained and ubiquitous that we don't even notice them anymore. Entitlement is a disgusting disease that destroys our ability to reach our dreams—because the exact moment entitlement engages is the same moment our self-discipline disengages.

> The exact moment entitlement engages is the same moment our self-discipline disengages.

Entitlement gets us nothing; only action does. I'm not saying I don't want your life to be easy. I do! But ease, comfort, and true satisfaction come through action. They come through working harder than you ever have before. They come from making more sacrifices, getting more done, being more focused, being more frugal, being more prudent, and being more committed. If you don't believe me, find the nearest successful person and ask them!

Entitlement is the end of achievement. Reject it. Get busy doing something that matters with your life, and you'll wake up one day with the rewards of success, even more than you ever thought you deserved.

PERFECTIONISM

Psychologists say that the number one cause of all procrastination is self-criticism. It can feel safer not to begin a daunting journey or not to take on a challenging task because at least we know we won't fail.

So instead of working, we wait. We wait for the perfect plan, the perfect time, and the perfect resources. The problem is, the perfect circumstances never show up. What was once a harmless decision of opting for safety soon becomes a limiting, even debilitating lifestyle of inaction.

The irony of this crippling fear of making mistakes is that mistakes can be our greatest teachers. No one has all the answers before they start. Successful people take action despite not knowing how it

> What was once a harmless decision of opting for safety soon becomes a limiting, even debilitating lifestyle of inaction.

will turn out, and they embrace the idea that success is messy along the way. They choose to move forward without knowing exactly where their path will lead, and they become comfortable with imperfection for the short term. They move. They go. They act.

Is perfectionism holding you back? Cultivate the habit of action in your life by being relentless about making progress, while letting go of the demand for perfection. You overcome perfectionism by insisting not on stellar results, but on stellar effort. Hold yourself to those standards, and your success is guaranteed.

360-Degree Accountability

If you're thinking this sounds like a tough and lonely journey, here's the good news. Through our coaching and consulting, we've seen for ourselves what psychologists have long known: People excel the most with the interest and support of others around them.

You've surely experienced this yourself—on both sides of the dynamic. We try harder, endure longer, and bounce back from disappointments faster when the people we care about take an interest in what we're doing. It's strange how easy it can be to let ourselves down, but how unbearable it can feel to let down others. At a fundamental level, we need each other—to motivate, empathize, push, challenge, and celebrate. In short, we have the power to help each other change our lives.

> It's strange how easy it can be to let ourselves down, but how unbearable it can feel to let down others.

We need community. We thrive off of partnership. It's why people hire coaches and trainers; it's why we take classes and find mentors; it's one of the ways family and friends can lend support and meaning to our lives.

In our coaching work, we help clients set up what we call 360-Degree Accountability. It's based on a simple principle: If you want to do everything to influence the likelihood of your taking action, it's important to have accountability in at least four different relationships, as follows:

- Supervisor: a boss or highly respected mentor
- Subordinate: an employee or mentee
- Significant other: a spouse, family member, colleague, best friend, or other trusted peer
- Supporter: a more objective outside third-party partner who will bring a unique unbiased perspective

(To inquire about our accountability program, please visit www .takethestairsbook.com/accountability.)

360-Degree Accountability works because each of these relationships has power. There is a powerful and significant *cost* in letting each of these people down. Also the cost of getting accountability in the form of a trainer, advisor, or coach may be a few hundred dollars a month, but the cost of no accountability is almost always immeasurably high. A good friend of mine who is in great shape once told me that any extra money he spends on expensive health food or workout equipment he just

> The cost of accountability may be a few hundred dollars a month, but the cost of no accountability is almost always immeasurably high.

considers to be a "six-pack tax." It's worth the investment on the front end to have what we want in the long term.

Create accountability in your life. Share your vision with someone who can encourage you, develop action plans with people who can help you, invest in your dream —and you'll be amazed at how quickly your fear, entitlement, and perfectionism begin to fade.

Call to Action

Although in our escalator world we'd rather try to find a way around it, action is the inevitable prerequisite for our success. Action validates our words; it erases our setbacks and cures our fears.

Action is the inevitable prerequisite for our success.

We cannot wait for the escalators of ease and convenience to show up in our life because the cost of that convenience is too great. With each ticking of the clock, the likelihood of my engaging toward the direction of greatness continues to wane. Often it is not making the *wrong decision* that has the greatest cost, but choosing *indecision* that does. Therefore, we have to reject ambivalent meandering and take control of what we can control. We have to own our circumstances, be responsible for our outcomes, and charge confidently into taking whatever actions are immediately available to us today.

You must develop the lifestyle of action. You must commit to action. You must embrace action. If you act, if you do, if you move, then you can have anything that you want. If you do not act, then you understand but you do not believe. If you do not act, you are merely an informed derelict. If you do not act, you are an unfortunate harbor of unused potential. If you do not act, if you do not do, if you do not move, then you shall not have.

You will act. You will win.

___

For corresponding videos for this chapter, visit www .takethestairsbook.com/pendulumprinciple.

FINAL NOTE: TIME TO CLIMB

The truth about success may not be popular, but it is certain. It may not be easy, but it is simple. In fact, it's so obvious that it can be elusive. And while it may not be what we want to hear about success, it is the only guaranteed method of high performance in any endeavor. It can all be summed up in one simple word . . . discipline.

The challenges we face today are not a matter of skill, but a matter of will. Our problem isn't time management; it is self-management. And we're not losing to poor circumstances as much as we're losing to a lack of self-discipline.

Yet you were born with an incredible power. You were born for a specific purpose. Inside you there is greatness that is indelibly yours. Your life matters a great deal, and regardless of what you've done right or wrong in the past, you have a chance to start making simple choices today that will enable you to have wild extravagant success far beyond what you ever thought possible in the future.

My hope is that this book has rejuvenated *your* hope in a truth that will modify your thoughts, influence your behaviors, and inevitably change your life. I know that this is a message that has been all but completely forgotten in our escalator world of instant, free, and easy. But I promise you that if you adopt these principles into your mind-set, they will change your life. They have certainly changed mine.

Beyond changing your own life, I hope that your actions will contagiously inspire those around you. After all, we are all accountable to each other, and your example, interest, and support will provide the essential accountability for the people you care about most. Our commitment to our dreams and to one another is ultimately responsible for shaping the world in which we all live. Taking the stairs together is all the more invigorating—and yes, even fun.

Thank you for embarking on this journey with me. If you commit to it every day, then discipline will never be as hard as it is right now. When you let go of the escalator world's "short-term-fix mentality" and instead adopt the mind-set that success is never owned, it is only rented—and the rent is due every day—then something truly magical happens. And that is that over time your appetite will begin to change. An empowering transformation occurs where you start to crave the things that you once couldn't get yourself to do, and the things that were once a great sacrifice to give up later won't even be temptations. When you embrace self-discipline as a conscious choice, it's not a source of sacrifice at all, but one of satisfaction. I look forward to continuing the journey together. See you in the "stairwell."

READERS GUIDE

Below you'll find discussion questions and action steps for each chapter in this book. I hope these questions and suggestions will reinforce the central principles, help you stay focused, and inspire you to strengthen and renew your commitment to taking the stairs.

Introduction: Waking Up in a ProcrastiNation

1. In what ways are you currently "taking the stairs" in your life? In what ways are you currently not taking the stairs?

2. Do you think that the "escalator mentality" is as pervasive as it's made out to be in this chapter? Is it possible to live

in a world where everyone is self-disciplined? What would that look like?

3. Do you agree that "success is never owned, it is only rented; and the rent is due every day"? Why, or why not? What invisible finish lines have you been chasing?

ACTION ITEM: This week, pay attention to the situations and choices you're confronted with that lead you to feel attracted toward the "escalator."

1. Sacrifice: The Paradox Principle

1. Can you think of examples from your own life when procrastinating made a situation or problem much worse? What could you have done differently?

2. What is procrastination costing you in your life? What are all the various ways that it "costs" you something?

3. When you apply the trajectory test to your habits and choices right now, what do you think your life will look like in twenty years if nothing changes?

ACTION ITEM: Write out a description of what you want your life to look like five years from now. Be as specific as possible.

2. Commitment: The Buy-In Principle

1. What commitments do you currently have in your life where the consequences of failing are so great that failure is simply not an option?
2. How could you increase your "investment" in the commitments?
3. Do you agree that there is often more emotional energy expended in making a decision than there is physical energy in executing the decision? Why or why not? What examples can you think of from your past experience?

ACTION ITEM: Make a list of all the things in your life that are "should-do's" and identify which ones are important enough to be converted into "How will I do's?"

3. Focus: The Magnification Principle

1. What are the most deceptive forms of distraction in your life right now?
2. Do you think you suffer from creative avoidance? If so, when does it set in?
3. How has "Mr. Mediocrity" impacted your life? In what positive or negative ways has he shown up?

ACTION ITEM: Write out ten positive affirmations that you can read to yourself (either silently or out loud) when "Mr. Mediocrity" starts acting up.

4. Integrity: The Creation Principle

1. Is there a lot of gossip surrounding the lives of those people closest to you? What could you do to lessen its impact, or even resolve the situation?
2. Are there people in your life whose words lift you up? Or bring you down? Whom do you admire, respect, and want to be most like?
3. Are there any examples in your life where you can clearly remember the pattern of "You think it, you speak it, you act, it happens"?

ACTION ITEM: Make a vision board by cutting out inspiring images from magazines and pasting them onto a poster board. Get creative, and don't worry about how it will look to others. This board is meant to inspire *you*.

5. Schedule: The Harvest Principle

1. What "season" is your life currently in? What other seasons have you recently completed? Are there any seasons that you foresee coming up soon?

2. Out of the Fundamental Five (Faith, Family, Fitness, Faculty, and Finances), which areas of your life are working the best? Which ones need the most work?

3. Do you think that you most often tie your self-esteem to results or to your work habits and effort?

ACTION ITEM: Write out a detailed schedule of what your ideal week would look like right now and also what your ideal week would look like in five years.

6. Faith: The Perspective Principle

1. Looking back on past experiences, can you think of examples of things that really didn't seem to be working out at the time, but that now, with the benefit of a different perspective, you feel good about?

2. How often do you view day-to-day setbacks, challenges, and frustrations with a long-term perspective? Do you ever have difficulty doing this? Why or why not?

3. How much peace are you experiencing in your life right now? What could you do that would give you more peace? What things cause you strife and worry?

ACTION ITEM: Approach someone in your life who appears to be frustrated with a current problem or setback. See if you can listen deeply, and work subtly and sensitively to broaden the term of their perspective.

7. Action: The Pendulum Principle

1. How has the Law of Diminishing Intent shown up in your life? Is there anything in your life that is currently victim to this concept?
2. Of the three emotional diseases of inaction (fear, entitlement, and perfectionism), which do you struggle with the most? Why do you think that is?
3. Other than yourself, who is holding you accountable to your goals? What is your game plan for increasing your accountability?

ACTION ITEM: Make a list of five things you know you could do (no matter how small) that would begin you down the path toward your dream.

Final Note: Time to Climb

1. What has been your most powerful personal insight from reading this book?
2. What things are you committed to changing in your life now that you know the truth about self-discipline and "overnight success"?
3. Who do you know that needs to read this book or hear this message?

ACTION ITEM: Share the answer to Question 1 with someone close to you and tell them what you learned from reading this book.

For more information about having Rory Vaden speak at your next event, to find out where you can see him live, or to get free updates, tips, and videos, please go to www.roryvaden.com.

If you would like to be considered for our accountability-coaching program, please apply at www.takethestairs book.com/accountability.

ACKNOWLEDGMENTS

God, please use me each day.
Make me a steward of the resources you've given me.
A fiduciary of the skills you've blessed me with.
A conduit for your message to pass.

To Mom, Dad, Randy, Sean, Letty, Jim, and all my family and friends, thank you for believing in me long before anyone else ever did. Thank you for your unconditional love!

To AJ, Dustin, Dave, Emmie, Gary, Lars, Stuart, Alan, Dan, Henry, Cindy, Melody, and the unstoppable team at Southwestern Consulting, thank you for your unconditional hard work, your ability to see vision in darkness, and your relentless commitment to making this world a better place.

To the Tillemans, Phillips, Kahles, Etzels, Oisters, Cruzes, and Martiens, thank you for being a part of our family and for helping us when we needed it most. I wouldn't be doing what I'm doing without you. I love you!

To Ms. Zulauf, Mrs. Kunches, Mr. Witty, Mrs. McElroy, Mr. Asmus, Mrs. Mitchell, Mrs. Stanford, Mrs. Kava, and the rest of my teachers, and to all schoolteachers and administrators everywhere, thank you for the life you dedicated to educating the next generation.

What you do matters. You are important and our humanity owes you a debt of gratitude.

To everyone at the Southwestern Family of Companies and all of our alumni, thank you for showcasing that truth still exists in the world and thank you for demonstrating your belief in building companies by building people. Each of you changes lives and creates an incalculable contribution to the world. I hope you will be pleased with this book as a small statement of who we are.

To Eric Chester, Dave Avrin, Mark Sanborn, Robert Smith, Marian Lizzi, Tracy Johnson, and Nena Madonia, there is simply no way this dream would have ever manifested without you. You had no reason to help me; but you did. I'll never be able to repay you but hopefully this work is honoring to you. You have no idea how much I look up to you. Thank you, Dave, for being a genius and for mentoring me through the creation and ideation of the Take the Stairs message and brand.

To Marshall Mathers, Mark Hall, Kelly Clarkson, and all the wide variety of artists who inspire me, thanks for helping me believe anything is possible.

To all the authors who are directly or indirectly referred to in this book, thank you for your wisdom and for allowing me to revisit some of your brilliance in relating it to self-discipline.

To Darren LaCroix, Ed Tate, Craig Valentine, David Brooks, Mark Brown, and Jim Key, thanks for paving a path for me, guys—and then sharing with me exactly what it takes to walk down it.

To my fellow Toastmasters and also my colleagues at the National Speakers Association, please keep your uplifting spirit. You are two of the most amazing organizations in the world and you change lives each and every day.

To my friends and faculty at the University of Denver and especially Colleen Hillmeyer, thank you for taking a chance on investing in me, for making one of my dreams come true, and for giving me the opportunity to receive the foundation of a first-class higher education.

Acknowledgments

To the amazing students and District Sales Leaders of the Southwestern student program, you are a collection of the best and brightest and you are our hope for the future . . . keep going. The answer is behind the next door.

To the hundreds of people who ever told me yes, thank you for the chance, the money, the support, and the confidence.

To the tens of thousands of people who ever told me no, thank you for the character. You made me who I am today.

ABOUT THE SOUTHWESTERN
FAMILY OF COMPANIES

In 1868, the Southwestern Company began working with college students to help them finance their way through school by training them to sell Bibles and other books door-to-door during their summers. Over the last 150 years, the company has remained true to that core business, although they now sell a subscription-based web product called the Southwestern Advantage. The Southwestern Advantage is an integrated learning system of books and a website that supplements what kids learn in school, helps parents help their kids with homework, and instills the kinds of life principles contained in this book. To eventually help reach every child in North America, Southwestern gives away a subscription for each one sold by students.

Working with Southwestern is one of the most challenging and rigorous opportunities a young person can become involved with. It is a comprehensive professional sales, entrepreneurship, and leadership training program. Average first-summer students make a gross profit of $8,500 and it's not uncommon for experienced dealers to make more than $30,000 each summer. Alumni of Southwestern include: Marsha Blackburn (U.S. congresswoman from Tennessee), Max Lucado (best-selling author), Jeff Sessions (U.S. senator from Alabama), Rick Perry (governor of Texas), Ronnie Musgrove (former governor of Mississippi), Mac Anderson (founder and former owner of Successories), Bruce Henderson (founder of Boston Consulting Group), Chinh Chu (senior managing director with The Blackstone Group), Donna Keene (former chief of staff for the Department of Education), and thousands more.

Today, in addition to the Southwestern student program, the company has thirteen partner companies in their corporate umbrella all specializing in some form of professional direct sales. They sell everything from custom tailored suits (Tom James); to supplemental insurance (Family Heritage); to financial planning (Southwestern Investments/Raymond James); to school fund-raising services (Great American Opportunities); to professional placement services (SBR); to all-natural food products through home parties (Wildtree); to professional sales and leadership training, coaching, and consulting (our company, Southwestern Consulting). Altogether the Southwestern family of companies has more than 4 million customers a year and generates more than $350 million in revenues.

To learn more about the Southwestern Company's summer program for college students, please visit www.takethestairsbook.com/south western.

ABOUT THE AUTHOR

Rory Vaden is a self-discipline strategist, author, and business motivational speaker whose insights have been shared on Oprah Radio and in *Businessweek* and *Success* magazines. Rory has degrees in business management, leadership, and an MBA. He is also the cofounder of the multimillion-dollar international training company Southwestern Consulting. As a two-time World Champion of public speaking finalist for Toastmasters International, Rory has shared his compelling Take the Stairs message on the same stage as John Maxwell, David Allen, and Keith Ferrazzi, and he's done special programs for Zig Ziglar's and Dave Ramsey's companies. His speaking and consulting client list includes Bank of America, Trane, Morgan Stanley Smith Barney, Shaw Worldwide, the Direct Selling Association, UnitedHealthcare, Mary Kay, and dozens of others from all over the world.

Rory is also leading a rapidly growing international social movement called the Take the Stairs World Tour in which he is raising charity money for youth character education programs by climbing stairs all over the place, including the ten tallest buildings in the world. Combining a hilarious and compelling delivery with unprecedented expertise, Rory energizes audiences into action with his signature program, "Take the Stairs: Success Means Doing Things You Don't Want to Do."